FINDING FAVOR

with

MAN

#1 *NEW YORK TIMES* BESTSELLING AUTHOR

MIKE EVANS

TIMEWORTHY
BOOKS

P.O. BOX 30000, PHOENIX, AZ 85046

This book is dedicated to
President Shimon Peres,
the international chair of the
Friends of Zion Heritage Center,
and a man whom I am pleased
to call my friend.

PART ONE: The Flavor of Favor

PART TWO: The Characteristics of Favor

PART ONE

THE FLAVOR
OF FAVOR

So you will find favor and good success
in the sight of God and man.

(PROVERBS 3:4 ESV)

INTRODUCTION

FINDING FAVOR WITH MAN is the third in a trilogy of books on supernatural favor in the life of a Believer. The first was *Living in the F.O.G. (Favor of God)*. It detailed how we, as children of God, can have His favor at work in our lives. After the release of that book, I began to ponder the question: What is favor *with* God, and does that differ from the favor *of* God? That led to the second book, *Finding Favor With God*.

With those two books came the realization that when we live in the F.O.G. and have favor with God, it leads to supernatural favor with man—overwhelming open doors, breathtaking blessings, awe-inspiring advantages, and unexpected returns.

Throughout my life in international ministry, God has opened doors that seemed to be firmly locked. As I've looked back at the God-given opportunities, I immediately thought of one particular meeting that took place in Jerusalem.

Several years ago, I was invited to meet with one of the most brilliant mathematicians in the world, Professor Robert J. (Israel) Aumann. In 2005, Professor Aumann won the Nobel Memorial Prize in Economic Sciences. Because he is such a busy individual, I was informed by his assistant that our meeting would last only fifteen minutes.

As I drove to the professor's home, I prayed that the Holy Spirit would give me favor, specifically with this one man: Israel Aumann. I said, "Lord, I have equity but no currency. I have enjoyed some influence with others, but I have no favor with *this* man. Would you convert what little I have into supernatural favor?"

As we met together, I asked him a question about the news. I was astonished to find that Professor Aumann had not watched television, listened to the radio, or read a newspaper since 1972. He said, "I do not put into my mind anything that is not relative to its objectives." Once a day, he was given a briefing paper with anything noteworthy.

During our time, I asked him one question that seemed to intrigue him: "Professor, you are a man of faith and a man of science. Can you tell me how those two things coexist so comfortably in a world where scholarship often rejects faith?"

"That is an excellent question," he remarked. "It's a tragedy that I don't have enough time to answer it. When I gave five days of lectures in Oslo, that was one of my topics. Neither I nor my smartest student could calculate where it could be found on the transcript. It was not printed. It was just a verbal lecture. It is in a computer somewhere."

As he walked me to the door after our brief meeting and I stepped outside, the professor said, "Breathe deeply." As I did, he said, "You've just breathed in about sixteen atoms that were exhaled from the mouth of Jesus on the cross. I've calculated the time and density."

I turned to walk away and muttered, "Twenty twenty-nine."

Mr. Aumann stopped me. "What did you say? It sounded like two numbers."

I replied, "Oh, it is probably just jet lag." He continued to prod until I responded, "I don't think it's anything more than that," but I repeated the numbers to him.

"Imagine," he said. "What if it began precisely at the top of page twenty and ended precisely at the bottom of page twenty-nine? This would be absolutely impossible for any man to deduce."

He became so intrigued that he invited me back inside and had his personal assistant contact Oslo. He discovered that was exactly what had happened. The lecture began on page 20 and ended on page 29. He turned to his aide and said, "Cancel my appointments. I'm going to spend the morning with Dr. Evans."

I said, "I don't think you want to do that. I don't know a thing about mathematics. The only thing I did as I was driving to your home was ask the Holy Spirit to give me favor with you."

He cried, "Mathematics! I'm not clearing my schedule to discuss mathematics. I'm clearing my schedule because there is a new field of science that has never been researched—the field of how the *Ruach HaKodesh* [Hebrew for "God's breath" or the Holy Spirit] can activate the cerebral mind to come up with such genius."

God has opened other doors for me with men and women such as Israeli prime ministers Menachem Begin, Shimon Peres, Yitzhak Rabin, Ehud Olmert, Benjamin Netanyahu; others such as Maureen Reagan, the daughter of Ronald Reagan; Ann Murchison, wife of the former owner of the Dallas Cowboys; Yoweri Museveni, president of Uganda, and numerous world leaders.

As you read this book, you will find other examples of God's great blessing of opening doors in my life; blessings you, too, can enjoy as you walk in the Favor of God. Why am I so convinced of this? It is because of the scripture in Luke 2, verse 52, "And Jesus increased in wisdom and stature, and in favor with God and men." Proverbs 16:7 says, "When a man's ways please the LORD, He makes even his enemies to be at peace with him."

How can we please God? How can we find favor with man? How can we conduct our lives in order to maximize that favor? I believe you will discover the answers to these questions in the pages of this book, *Finding Favor With Man.*

CHAPTER ONE

FINDING FAVOR WITH MAN MEANS LIVING TO PLEASE GOD

Let not mercy and truth forsake you; bind them around your neck, write them on the tablet of your heart, and so find favor and high esteem in the sight of God and man. Trust in the LORD with all your heart, and lean not on your own understanding; in all your ways acknowledge Him, and He shall direct your paths.

— PROVERBS 3:3–6

TOO MANY TIMES in a Believer's life, temptation to follow the crowd arises. Situations and circumstances produce opportunities to walk down a contrary path. One such set of circumstances presented itself at my mother's funeral. Having been notified of her death, I flew to Boston and then drove to Springfield, Massachusetts, to join my family for her funeral. I arrived at her home only to discover that one of my siblings had unsuccessfully attempted to have her interred before my arrival.

These efforts had not stopped there: Whatever money could be found was spent on alcohol and drugs; one had even managed to purchase a new car. As I walked into my mother's house, I encountered a group of people high on drugs and with a beer party in full swing. My mother's body was at the funeral home awaiting burial. Rather than having a quick funeral, the decision had been made to delay her burial indefinitely; no one wanted to spend the money for the funeral. Needless to say, I was furious.

The choice before me was: live to please my family and join my siblings in their revelry, or live to please God and remove myself from that setting. Instantly, everything came into focus. I knew who the Enemy was, and I knew what had to be done. Quickly, leaving my siblings in the living room, I walked upstairs to the room where, at the age of eleven, I had encountered Jesus. There I knelt down and prayed: *Jesus, it was in this room that You appeared to me. You told me You loved me. God, my mother is dead. Now what are You going to do?*

Instantly He brought two scriptures to mind. The first was 2 Timothy 1:7:

> For God has not given us a spirit of fear, but of power and of love and of a sound mind.

Then He reminded me of the verse that says:

> The LORD directs the steps of the godly. He delights in every detail of their lives (Psalm 37:23 NLT).

The Spirit of God whispered, *"Who* really *killed your mother? Who is causing all the problems?"*

Kneeling in prayer, I realized that I did not have to operate in the spirit of fear, but could rely wholly on God's power, and love, and His provision for a sound mind.

As I arose and descended the stairs to stand in the midst of my family, I said, "You will be saved! God is coming for you." As I watched them stagger around the room, I felt in a sense what the Father must feel when we choose worldly pursuits over Him. I love my siblings, and it grieves my spirit that they continue to refuse to commit their lives to the living God. I can be confident, however, in Matthew 6:33 that says, "But seek first the kingdom of God and His righteousness, and all these things shall be added to you." When we seek God first, He will provide favor with man that doesn't require compromise in our spiritual values.

How can a Believer please God and position himself/herself for blessings of favor? Pledge to be totally committed to Him. Paul gave us a strategy in Romans 12:1:

> I beseech you therefore, brethren, by the mercies of God, that you present your bodies a living sacrifice, holy, acceptable to God, which is your reasonable service.

Surrender your plans, dreams, expectations, and yearnings to Jesus. The psalmist wrote in chapter 37, verse 5, "Commit your way to the LORD, trust also in Him, and He shall bring it to pass."

The life that is pleasing to our heavenly Father is one that is continually growing in grace, favor, and the knowledge of Him. This is not an exercise in how to get what you want from God; it is an exercise in intimacy with our Lord—in learning to love more deeply, to grow closer to Him.

The book of Nehemiah teaches a beautiful lesson on how to grow closer to God and reap the wonderful blessings He has reserved for His children. After seventy years of captivity in Babylon, God touched the heart of Cyrus the Great, who began to allow the Israelites to return to Jerusalem.

Nehemiah, a captive Jew and cupbearer to the king, held an important and trusted position in the royal court. He had been deemed so exceedingly loyal as to be allowed to serve drinks to the king. He could at any given moment be asked to take a sip of the wine to ensure that it was free of poison.

In chapter 1, Nehemiah is approached by a group of his brethren from Judah, bearers of bad news:

> And they said to me, "The survivors who are left from the captivity in the province are there in great distress and reproach. The wall of Jerusalem is also broken down, and its gates are burned with fire" (v. 3).

Nehemiah's response was immediate; he turned to Jehovah:

> So it was, when I heard these words, that I sat down and wept, and mourned for many days; I was fasting and praying before the God of heaven. And I said: "I pray, LORD God of heaven, O great and awesome God, You who keep Your covenant and mercy with those who love You and observe Your commandments, please let Your ear be attentive and Your eyes open, that You may hear the prayer of Your servant which I pray before You now, day and night, for the children of Israel Your servants, and confess the sins of the children of Israel which we have sinned against You. Both my father's house and I have sinned. We

have acted very corruptly against You, and have not kept the commandments, the statutes, nor the ordinances which You commanded Your servant Moses. Remember, I pray, the word that You commanded Your servant Moses, saying, 'If you are unfaithful, I will scatter you among the nations; but if you return to Me, and keep My commandments and do them, though some of you were cast out to the farthest part of the heavens, yet I will gather them from there, and bring them to the place which I have chosen as a dwelling for My name.' Now these are Your servants and Your people, whom You have redeemed by Your great power, and by Your strong hand. O Lord, I pray, please let Your ear be attentive to the prayer of Your servant, and to the prayer of Your servants who desire to fear Your name; and let Your servant prosper this day, I pray, and grant him mercy in the sight of this man."

Author W. F. Adeney wrote:

> The brief and sudden prayer reaches heaven as an arrow shot from the bow, but it goes right home, because he who lets it off in his surprise is a good workman, well-practiced. This ready prayer only springs to the lips of a man who lives in a daily habit of praying.[1]

Nehemiah prayed for favor with King Artaxerxes, and then proceeded to do his job in the court. He made no plans; he plotted no drastic measures to gain the king's attention; he simply went about his duties daily suffused with prayer. But as Nehemiah prayed and contemplated the news that had been delivered from Jerusalem, he could not mask his despair over what had befallen his beloved city. (See Nehemiah 1:1–3.)

> Now I had never been sad in his [the king's] presence before. Therefore the king said to me, "Why is your face sad, since you are not sick? This is nothing but sorrow of heart." So I became dreadfully afraid, and said to the king, "May the king live forever! Why should my face not be sad, when the city, the place of my fathers' tombs, lies waste, and its gates are burned with fire?" Then the king said to me, "What do you request?" So I prayed to the God of heaven. And I said to the king, "If it pleases the king, and if your servant has found favor in your sight, I ask that you send me to Judah, to the city of my fathers' tombs, that I may rebuild it" (Nehemiah 2:1–5).

Nehemiah was then blessed with great favor by Artaxerxes, who allowed him to return to Jerusalem, not as a casual traveler, but as an emissary of the king. Artaxerxes generously provided safe passage and materials sufficient not only to rebuild the wall surrounding the city and the Temple, but to provide a home for Nehemiah during his stay in Judah.

The cupbearer's response in verse 8 was one of gratitude:

> And the king granted them [his requests] to me according to the good hand of my God upon me.

So Nehemiah undertook the two-month journey from Susa to Jerusalem to observe the appalling condition of the walls surrounding the city and the Temple within those broken-down walls. The last part of a quote attributed to Dallas cosmetics businesswoman, the late Mary Kay Ash, defines Nehemiah:

> There are three types of people in this world: those who make things happen, those who watch things happen, and those who wonder what happened.[2]

Nehemiah's prayer and intercession had touched the heart of God, turned His head, and moved His hand. Jehovah had given him favor, and in doing so, blessed the Jews who remained in Jerusalem. Now the cupbearer was ready to go to work and make things happen.

Once in the city, Nehemiah found that the people "had a mind to work" (4:6). The job was not without peril, for at every step the Israelites were challenged by those who had no desire to see righteousness rise in the land. We read in Nehemiah 4:17–20 just how difficult the task was:

> Those who built on the wall, and those who carried burdens, loaded themselves so that with one hand they worked at construction, and with the other held a weapon. Every one of the builders had his sword girded at his side as he built. And the one who sounded the trumpet was beside me. Then I said to the nobles, the rulers, and the rest of the people, "The work is great and extensive, and we are separated far from one another on the wall. Wherever you hear the

sound of the trumpet, rally to us there. Our God will fight for us."

Nearing the completion of the rebuilding and re-population of Jerusalem, Nehemiah realized there was one void that had not been filled—a spiritual barrenness that could not be satisfied with stone and timber.

The cupbearer-turned-architect began at once to fortify the Israelites with the Word of God. As had Jeremiah, Nehemiah knew the value of repentance and return:

> Thus says the LORD: "Stand in the ways and see, and ask for the old paths, where the good way is, and walk in it; then you will find rest for your souls" (Jeremiah 6:16).

On the first day of the seventh month following completion of the work, Nehemiah called the people together before the Water Gate. Ezra, the scribe, brought the Book of the Law of Moses, climbed atop a scaffold, and began to read the Word. Now all the people gathered together as one man in the open square that was in front of the Water Gate; and they told Ezra the scribe to bring the Book of the Law of Moses, which the LORD had commanded Israel. As they listened to Ezra read from the scroll, "all the people wept, when they heard the words of the Law" (See Nehemiah 8:9.)

In his study on the book of Nehemiah, Donald K. Campbell wrote:

> It is noteworthy also that "the ears of all the people were attentive unto the book of the Law" (v. 3b). The

people had arisen very early and listened patiently hour after hour to the reading of the Scripture. Many of them had not heard the Word of God for many years; some had probably not heard it at all. It was a spiritual feast for their hungry souls as they sat in rapt attention. No wonder a work of God would soon be accomplished in their midst. A New Testament parallel is found in the dramatic scene where Cornelius and his household said to Peter, "Now therefore are we all here present before God, to hear all things that are commanded thee of God" (Acts 10:33.) And a significant work of grace followed.[3]

I am reminded of a passage in Isaiah 55:11:

So shall My word be that goes forth from My mouth; it shall not return to Me void, but it shall accomplish what I please, and it shall prosper *in the thing* for which I sent it.

The Word was read and it did indeed bring repentance, restoration, and revival. The people bowed their faces to the ground and worshipped Jehovah in submission to His authority. When you and I determine to surrender our will to His, our Lord responds with love, mercy, and favor—with God and man.

On June 17, 1843, the great orator Daniel Webster delivered a speech at the celebration of the completion of the Bunker Hill Monument in Boston. In his speech, he addressed the importance of the Word of God:

The English colonists in America, generally speaking, were men who were seeking new homes in a new world. They brought with them their families and all that was most dear to them . . . . They brought with them a full portion of all the riches of the past, in science, in art, in morals, religion, and literature. The Bible came with them. And it is not to be doubted, that to the free and universal reading of the Bible, in that age, men were much indebted for right views of civil liberty. The Bible is a book of faith, and a book of doctrine, and a book of morals, and a book of religion, of especial revelation from God; but it is also a book which teaches man his own individual responsibility, his own dignity, and his equality with his fellow-man.[4]

How can we please our heavenly Father as we walk daily with Him? We can live in obedience to Him and to His Word. We can be doers of the Word as the apostle Paul wrote in James 1:22: "But be doers of the word, and not hearers only, deceiving yourselves." We must put into practice those things we read in the Word.

We must be motivated to follow Christ, to measure everything we do or say by the yardstick of the Bible. During the 1990s a popular question sprang up among Evangelicals: What would Jesus do? Bracelets, caps, T-shirts, and jewelry sported the initials "WWJD." It was to be a reminder of the moral constraint to conduct oneself in a manner that would be pleasing to God. It was a call to permit love for Jesus to control our actions, transform our lives, and therefore please God in all that we do and say. It was to be the living out of Romans 12:2:

And do not be conformed to this world, but be transformed by the renewing of your mind, that you may prove what *is* that good and acceptable and perfect will of God.

This is a relationship with Jehovah that will be transforming, invigorating, and uplifting. It will be pleasing to God and will produce favor—with God and man.

—DISCUSSION—
MATERIAL

1. How can a Believer please God and position himself/herself for blessings of favor?

2. How can we please our heavenly Father as we walk daily with Him?

3. When Nehemiah heard of the plight of his people in Jerusalem and the state of the city, what did he do?

4. Consider why prayer should be our first action and not our last resort.

5. Why is it important that we measure our every action by the yardstick of the Word of God?

—SCRIPTURES ON—
LIVING TO PLEASE GOD

And whatsoever we ask, we receive of him, because we keep his commandments, and do those things that are pleasing in his sight.

1 JOHN 3:22

For they that are after the flesh do mind the things of the flesh; but they that are after the Spirit the things of the Spirit.

ROMANS 8:5

The Lord is not slack concerning his promise, as some men count slackness; but is longsuffering to us-ward, not willing that any should perish, but that all should come to repentance.

2 PETER 3:9

But to do good and to communicate forget not: for with such sacrifices God is well pleased.

HEBREWS 13:16

Fulfil ye my joy, that ye be likeminded, having the same love, being of one accord, of one mind.

PHILIPPIANS 2:2

And to love him with all the heart, and with all the understanding, and with all the soul, and with all the strength, and to love his neighbour as himself, is more than all whole burnt offerings and sacrifices.

MARK 12:33

I beseech you therefore, brethren, by the mercies of
God, that ye present your bodies a living sacrifice, holy,
acceptable unto God, which is your reasonable service.
And be not conformed to this world: but be ye transformed
by the renewing of your mind, that ye may prove what is
that good, and acceptable, and perfect, will of God. For I
say, through the grace given unto me, to every man that
is among you, not to think of himself more highly than he
ought to think; but to think soberly, according as God hath
dealt to every man the measure of faith.

ROMANS 12:1–3

For I desired mercy, and not sacrifice; and the knowledge of
God more than burnt offerings.

HOSEA 6:6

CHAPTER TWO

OBEDIENCE
BEGETS FAVOR

*Obedience is better than sacrifice, and submission
is better than offering the fat of rams.*

—1 SAMUEL 15:22 NLT

AFTER MY CAB STOPPED in front of the Waldorf Astoria in New York City, I paid the driver and slid out of the back seat. The front door of the hotel where Iran's then president Mahmoud Ahmadinejad was staying was surrounded by what were obviously security types, and the doors were equipped with a metal detector. As I approached the group, I was amazed when one of the men motioned me through the door. Once inside the hotel, I noticed a man standing at the top of a short flight of stairs. The Holy Spirit whispered, *Go stand by that man.* I knew how Stephen must have felt when God told him to attach himself to the chariot of the Ethiopian. (See Acts 8:26–40.)

As I introduced myself, I was astounded to discover that I was standing next to the man in charge of protocol for a brunch with African heads of state. We chatted for a few minutes before I heard steps behind me. When I turned, I was staring into the face of my dear friend and Ugandan President Yoweri Musevani.

"Mike Evans!" the president cried with his hand extended. "What are you doing here? Wait, I know. God sent you, right? That's what you told me when you came to Uganda years ago."

"Mr. President, what a pleasure to see you again. Is your lovely wife, Janet, here with you?"

"No, other duties kept her at home this time."

"Please give her my regards. She was such a gracious hostess when we last met."

The chief of protocol cleared his throat. "Gentlemen, if you will step this way. We need to allow other guests to enter."

The president smiled. "Certainly. Mike, come with me. I want to know what you've been doing since our meeting."

"But, Mr. President, I'm not invited to the brunch. I won't be able to go with you."

"Mike, I've just invited you as my guest. Come on, before they give our seats to someone else."

After all these years, I am still amazed that when I obey the voice of the Holy Spirit, God grants me favor with men like President Musevani. Me, Michael Evans, the kid from the wrong side of the tracks, the kid who dug through the local dump for food, the abused and unloved little boy; and yet He has given me favor beyond comprehension.

Have you ever wondered why God chose Mary and Joseph to parent His only begotten Son? Perhaps for the same reason He chose Abraham, of whom He said:

> For I have chosen him, that he may command his
> children and his household after him to keep the

way of the LORD by doing righteousness and justice,
so that the LORD may bring to Abraham what he has
promised him (Genesis 18:19 ESV).

Jehovah recognized the attributes Mary and Joseph would bring to parenthood. They would train up this very special child in the way He should go. (See Proverbs 22:6.)

One small verse almost hidden in Luke 2:52 is an open window on the early life of Christ. It reads, "And Jesus increased in wisdom and stature, and in favor with God and men." At the age of twelve, Jesus had found favor with the teachers in the Temple. This scripture follows the Passover visit to Jerusalem by Mary, Joseph, and the twelve-year-old. At the conclusion of the feast, the family gathered its belongings and joined the crowd returning to Nazareth. After having traveled for a full day, the parents suddenly realized Jesus was not in the company of His friends. Apparently He was a trustworthy boy old enough to celebrate His first *bar mitzvah* and therefore His absence had not raised an alarm. Perhaps it was time for dinner when He was missed, and a frantic Mary and Joseph turned their donkey around and began the long journey back to Jerusalem. After three days of fear and anguish, of searching and longing, the parents found Jesus in the Temple court.

It is likely that Jesus stayed behind, not to cause pain to His parents, but from an insatiable desire for knowledge, and maybe for another reason altogether. It could be that the reason is found in Luke 2:48–50:

So when they saw Him, they were amazed; and
His mother said to Him, "Son, why have You done
this to us? Look, Your father and I have sought You

anxiously." And He said to them, "Why did you seek Me? Did you not know that I must be about My Father's business?" But they did not understand the statement which He spoke to them.

Rev. John Piper, Minneapolis teacher and seminarian, said of this event:

> They were searching and searching and finally they turn him up at the temple. Where did they search? In the playground, the local swimming hole, in the shops, at the bakery? Jesus answers: You shouldn't have had to seek at all. For you know, don't you, that there is laid on me an inner necessity to be in my Father's house (or about his business—either translation is possible)?[5]

Could it be that the young child was driving home a point that Mary had missed in her earlier Temple encounter with Simeon? The old man had warned the mother of Jesus that "yes, a sword will pierce through your own soul also" (Luke 2:35). The pages of Scripture are filled with types and shadows. Might not this be another example of a time that would come at the conclusion of Christ's ministry on the earth—when the Son of Man would be suspended on a cross between heaven and earth? When an anguished Mary would again stand vigil beneath the cross that held her son?

Jesus also grew in stature: He became grounded in education, physical health, moral teachings, and social interaction. Rather than proclaim to Joseph and Mary the importance of His mission and insist that He be allowed to begin His earthly ministry, Jesus humbled himself and went home to Nazareth. There He worked alongside Joseph in the carpenter shop, sat beside him in the synagogue, and learned obedience. It was early Christian theologian St. Augustine who said:

> He was created of a mother whom He created. He was carried by hands that He formed. He cried in the manger in wordless infancy, He the Word, without whom all human eloquence is mute.[6]

And yet His entire life was one of obedience, to His earthly parents and to His heavenly Father. In his letter to the Philippian church, Paul wrote:

> And being found in appearance as a man, He humbled Himself and became obedient to *the point of death, even the death of the cross,* (Philippians 2:8).

The favor of man is not easy to obtain or retain. People are capricious: One moment adoring, the next ready to destroy the beloved. And yet finding favor with man is important even for Christians as we try to traverse the rocky path before us. It doesn't mean that we are to compromise our beliefs in order to gain that favor; it simply means that we constantly seek to know what Jesus would do and follow His lead.

Have you ever known a Christian who worked diligently and enjoyed success beyond measure? Who seemed to lead a charmed life, finding favor with both God and man? My friend, luck has nothing to do with it. If you look more closely, you will likely find that the person in question is a tireless and dedicated servant of God.

Does it mean that the individual has never faced challenges or hard times? Not at all; it simply means that through the good times and bad, he or she has faithfully served God with the confidence that a loving heavenly Father would grant them favor with man and turn every problem into an opportunity for blessing.

When God grants favor with man, it can accomplish what personality, ability, talent, and exertion may not achieve. Such favor can open doors that might normally remain tightly closed and locked. It can create opportunities otherwise unavailable. The great buzzword of this decade is *networking*. It is a means to further one's career path, to meet people with like interests. God's favor is networking at its very best. So don't hesitate to pray for God's favor; but while you pray, walk uprightly before Him and extend grace and favor to those you meet along the way. Psalm 84:11 says, "For the LORD God is a sun and shield; the LORD will give grace and glory; no good thing will He withhold from those who walk uprightly." And that includes favor with man.

Second Peter 3:18 admonishes us to "grow in the grace and knowledge of our Lord and Savior Jesus Christ." And Colossians 1:9–10 says:

> For this reason we also, since the day we heard it, do not cease to pray for you, and to ask that you may be filled with the knowledge of His will in all wisdom and spiritual understanding; that you may walk worthy of the Lord, fully pleasing Him, being fruitful in every good work and increasing in the knowledge of God;

We see a clear picture of God's reaction to the parenting of Mary and Joseph as Jesus made His way to the Jordan River to be baptized by his cousin John:

> When He had been baptized, Jesus came up immediately from the water; and behold, the heavens were opened to Him, and He saw the Spirit of God descending like a dove and alighting upon Him. And suddenly a voice came from heaven, saying, "This is My beloved Son, in whom I am well pleased" (Matthew 3:16–17).

God the Father could immediately view the past thirty years of Jesus' life and put His stamp of approval on it. Here were diligence, love, submission, obedience, and an excellent work ethic—and God was pleased with what He saw.

Another picture of Christ's obedience to His earthly parents was His penchant for taking everyday events during His ministry and using them as illustrations—or parables. Perhaps it was Joseph and Mary who used those ordinary happenings to teach Jesus spiritual truths, whether it was cleaning house, mending clothing, sowing and reaping, or removing a splinter from a little boy's finger.

In an article written about the delightful 1950 movie *Harvey*, starring the late James Stewart, the main character, Elwood P. Dowd treated the audience to this bit of wisdom:

> Years ago my mother used to say to me, she'd say, "In this world, Elwood, you must be"—she always called me Elwood—"In this world, you must be oh so smart or oh so pleasant." Well, for years I was smart. I recommend pleasant. And you may quote me . . . .

As a college student at a fairly prestigious liberal arts school, it's very easy to get caught up in the stress of homework, essay writing, and exams."[7]

The article continued:

This quote, and this movie in general, is about seeing life from a different perspective and learning that how you treat people and yourself might be more important than simply being intelligent. I believe that Elwood . . . is very wise, even though he does not strive to be.

An example of this is how he interacts with everyone else in the movie—he's always kind, considerate, and polite, even when they are doing things that are not in his favor.[8]

Jesus, the obedient Son of God and Son of Man, was the epitome of kindness. He learned how to contend with people. He was not aloof but made himself available to those from every quarter of life—the poor, the wealthy, and even the despised tax collector who surely visited Joseph to collect the king's dues. This Jesus must have learned by helping Joseph in the carpenter shop. He was taught how to treat children and the elderly, the pious and the profane. He was accused of dining with publicans (tax collectors) and sinners. Yet He took every opportunity to teach the Word of God to those with whom He interacted, whether on the road, at the table, by the seashore, or in a garden.

—DISCUSSION—
MATERIAL

1. Why do you think God chose Mary
   and Joseph to parent His only begotten
   Son? Why would or why would you
   not have wanted to assume that
   responsibility?

2. Have you ever known someone who
   worked diligently and enjoyed success
   beyond measure? Who seemed to lead
   a charmed life, finding favor with both
   God and man?

3. Do you think God shows favoritism to
   His children? Why? Why not?

4. Relate a time when God granted you
   favor with man.

5. How do you picture Jesus as a child?

—SCRIPTURES ON—
OBEDIENCE

If ye love me, keep my commandments.
JOHN 14:15

And why call ye me, Lord, Lord, and do not the things
which I say?
LUKE 6:46

Know ye not, that to whom ye yield yourselves servants to
obey, his servants ye are to whom ye obey; whether of sin
unto death, or of obedience unto righteousness?
ROMANS 6:16

Not every one that saith unto me, Lord, Lord, shall enter
into the kingdom of heaven; but he that doeth the will of my
Father which is in heaven.
MATTHEW 7:21

But be ye doers of the word, and not hearers only, deceiving
your own selves.
JAMES 1:22

This book of the law shall not depart out of thy mouth; but
thou shalt meditate therein day and night, that thou mayest
observe to do according to all that is written therein: for
then thou shalt make thy way prosperous, and then thou
shalt have good success.
JOSHUA 1:8

Servants, be obedient to them that are your masters
according to the flesh, with fear and trembling, in
singleness of your heart, as unto Christ.
EPHESIANS 6:5

And Samuel said, Hath the LOR as great delight in burnt offerings and sacrifices, as in obeying the voice of the LORD? Behold, to obey is better than sacrifice, and to hearken than the fat of rams.

1 SAMUEL 15:22

Ye see then how that by works a man is justified, and not by faith only.

JAMES 2:24

And we know that all things work together for good to them that love God, to them who are the called according to his purpose.

ROMANS 8:28

In flaming fire taking vengeance on them that know not God, and that obey not the gospel of our Lord Jesus Christ.

2 THESSALONIANS 1:8

If ye be willing and obedient, ye shall eat the good of the land.

ISAIAH 1:19

And being made perfect, he became the author of eternal salvation unto all them that obey him.

HEBREWS 5:9

Because strait is the gate, and narrow is the way, which leadeth unto life, and few there be that find it.

MATTHEW 7:14

Put them in mind to be subject to principalities and powers, to obey magistrates, to be ready to every good work.

TITUS 3:1

CHAPTER THREE

PRAYER PRODUCES FAVOR

*The effective, earnest prayer of a righteous
man is powerfully effective.*

—JAMES 5:26 HNV

IN APRIL 1992, I was invited to El Salvador, a nation in the midst of a bloody civil war, to address a group of Christian Believers. Shortly after arrival, I went to my hotel room to spend some time in prayer. As I prayed, delegations began to arrive seeking a meeting with me—this even included leaders of the nation.

The following morning after breakfast with the Minister of the Interior, I felt God was instructing me to walk. As I headed for the front door of the hotel, the president of El Salvador, Alfredo Cristiani, entered the building. I approached him with my hand extended and, after chatting for a few minutes, was invited to meet with him in his office the following day. God had given me favor and opened a door with the leader of the nation.

During our conversation, I shared 2 Chronicles 7:14 with him:

> If My people who are called by My name will hum-
> ble themselves, and pray and seek My face, and turn
> from their wicked ways, then I will hear from heaven,
> and will forgive their sin and heal their land.

In our meeting were several generals and his secretary of state, who wrote the scripture on the palm of his hand. The country's civil war had claimed the lives of more than 75,000 people. Suddenly, groups began meeting to pray in city squares and parks all over San Salvador. The president drafted a proclamation to call the nation to prayer—and that was only the beginning.

Critics had declared we would not be able to fill a stadium, but the hand of God moved over the land, and large crowds gathered for prayer and the ministry of the Word.

One day the vice president's wife called and requested that I come to their home; she wanted prayer for an ailment. In the company of a group of men that included Dr. Jose Coto, a noted El Salvadoran surgeon, we left the hotel for her residence. As we were driven through the streets, I noticed a dirty beggar whose arms and legs were terribly twisted.

As we passed by him, the Holy Spirit whispered that I was to stop and pray for him; I ignored that still, small voice and went on my way. When our entourage reached the vice president's palace, I literally could not get out of the car. The Holy Spirit again whispered that I would not have His blessing to pray for the wife unless I obeyed His earlier directive. I turned to the driver and asked him to take me back to the square. The car halted before the crippled man and we got out. Dr. Coto and I walked up to him, and as had the apostle Peter, I said:

> Silver and gold I do not have, but what I do have
> I give you: In the name of Jesus Christ of Nazareth,
> rise up and walk, (Acts 3:6).

Instantly, the man's limbs were straightened and strengthened and he began to praise God as he jumped up and ran down the street. People in cars and along the sidewalk stopped as the man gave his amazing testimony of God's power to heal. We then returned to the vice president's home, where Dr. Coto and I anointed the second lady of El Salvador and prayed for her. It soon became evident that prayer and God's anointing produced favor for me among the peoples of the nation.

Acts chapter 16, verses 16–40 relates the story of the apostle Paul and his missionary traveling companion, Silas. The two men arrived in the city of Philippi and discovered there was no synagogue for them to attend. After some searching, Paul and Silas found a convert and were invited to stay with the family. Before long, the missionaries realized they were in deep trouble. Satan had recognized his adversaries and set a demon-possessed slave who was a fortune-teller for her owners on the trail of God's agents. She shadowed Paul and his colleague through the streets of the city derisively shouting, "These men are the servants of the Most High God, who proclaim to us the way of salvation." (See Acts 16:17.) Why was that a bad thing? The people were paying more attention to her caterwauling than to the actual message of salvation being preached by the two evangelists. In Acts 16:18 (NIV), we read Paul's response to the Enemy's interference:

> Finally Paul became so annoyed that he turned
> around and said to the spirit, "In the name of Jesus

Christ I command you to come out of her!" At that moment the spirit left her.

It was truly an "uh-oh, we've gone too far" moment as her owners realized they had lost their effortless income from her soothsaying. Not content to fold their tent and look for a more high-volume street corner, the slavers wanted revenge—with a capital *R*. As had their Lord been before them, Paul and Silas were dragged into the town square. The two men were dropped on the pavement at the feet of the magistrates and charged falsely:

> These men, being Jews, exceedingly trouble our
> city; and they teach customs which are not lawful for
> us, being Romans, to receive or observe (vv. 20–21).

Magistrates and crowd alike were whipped into a roaring frenzy; Paul and Silas were stripped of their outer garments and beaten before being thrown in prison. The two were forced into the inner prison and placed in stocks—often "a log or timber with holes in which the feet, hands, [and] neck of prisoners were inserted and fastened with thongs."[9]

I wonder what you or I might have done at that moment: scream, cry, whine, or perhaps blame God for our incarceration? Can you picture them there on that cold, dirty, rough stone floor? They were shackled, sore, and suffering from the battering they received. They had been forced into an excruciating position, bodies tormented by cramps, wounds oozing, and splinters from the roughhewn boards driven deep into their tender skin.

But at midnight Paul and Silas were praying and singing hymns to God, and the prisoners were listening to them (v. 25).

About that time, an earthquake rolled through the jail. This was not a minor aftershock; it was probably a full-bore 10 on the Richter scale. It was massive enough to throw open the doors of the cells, break open the stocks that bound the two brutalized prisoners, and rip their chains right out of the stone walls.

The other prisoners had been listening to Paul and Silas serenade them with praise-and-worship music from hearts filled with gratitude to their heavenly Father. Suddenly, they were free—cowering in a corner, but free. The terrified Philippian jailer rushed into the confines of the jail and, seeing no one, drew his sword with every intention of falling on it. He knew that had one prisoner escaped, he would have been held accountable and summarily executed.

The torches or lamps that would have illuminated the cells had likely been ripped from clefts in the rocks and had fizzled out once they hit the floor. Darkness hid the corners where the inmates recoiled. Perhaps by the light of the torch the jailer carried, Paul saw what the guard was about to do and shouted at him, "Do yourself no harm, for we are all here" (v. 28).

The jailer was speechless! Prisoners who sang praises when they were arrested and beaten, who stayed put when presented with an opportunity to flee into the darkness and chaos of the night. What was it about those two men? Startled by what he had heard, the warden called to other guards to bring lights to illuminate the dark, cavernous rooms. Apparently the words of the earlier songs had made an impression on the Philippian, for he threw himself down at the feet of Paul and Silas and cried out, "Sirs, what must I do to be saved?" (v. 30).

Without hesitation, a free man though still in pain, Paul answered simply and unhesitatingly, "Believe on the Lord Jesus Christ, and you will be saved, you and your household" (v. 31).

Prayers produced freedom and favor for the jailer, and at that very hour he "washed their stripes. And immediately he and all his family were baptized. Now when he had brought them into his house, he set food before them; and he rejoiced, having believed in God with all his household" (vv. 33–34).

There are numerous verses in the Bible that refer to favor for those who chose to follow the laws and precepts of God and were prayer warriors. Too often, Believers feel they must forfeit favor with man in order to follow God, but that is not supported in Scripture. The reverse is often true: Just as Jesus grew in favor with God and man, so can we when we walk in His ways.

—DISCUSSION—
MATERIAL

1. Paul and Silas had gone to Philippi to preach the gospel. There they encountered a young woman who followed them shouting that they were servants of God. Why was that upsetting to Paul and Silas?

2. Paul rebuked her, making her slave masters angry. What was the real reason they were so upset?

3. Paul and Silas were thrown into prison. Have you ever been unjustly accused and shunned by others? How did you react?

4. What did Paul and Silas do while in prison that was so out of the ordinary?

5. Did God give them favor in that situation? What was the result?

—SCRIPTURES ON—
PRAYER

Be careful for nothing; but in every thing by prayer and supplication with thanksgiving let your requests be made known unto God.
PHILIPPIANS 4:6

Pray without ceasing.
1 THESSALONIANS 5:17

Therefore I say unto you, What things soever ye desire, when ye pray, believe that ye receive them, and ye shall have them.
MARK 11:24

Praying always with all prayer and supplication in the Spirit, and watching thereunto with all perseverance and supplication for all saints.
EPHESIANS 6:18

Confess your faults one to another, and pray one for another, that ye may be healed. The effectual fervent prayer of a righteous man availeth much.
JAMES 5:16

Likewise the Spirit also helpeth our infirmities: for we know not what we should pray for as we ought: but the Spirit itself maketh intercession for us with groanings which cannot be uttered.
ROMANS 8:26

And all things, whatsoever ye shall ask in prayer, believing, ye shall receive.
MATTHEW 21:22

But when ye pray, use not vain repetitions, as the heathen do: for they think that they shall be heard for their much speaking.
MATTHEW 6:7

Continue in prayer, and watch in the same with thanksgiving.
COLOSSIANS 4:2

Evening, and morning, and at noon, will I pray, and cry aloud: and he shall hear my voice.
PSALM 55:17

Let us therefore come boldly unto the throne of grace, that we may obtain mercy, and find grace to help in time of need.
HEBREWS 4:16

Seek ye the LORD while he may be found, call ye upon him while he is near.
ISAIAH 55:6

If my people, which are called by my name, shall humble themselves, and pray, and seek my face, and turn from their wicked ways; then will I hear from heaven, and will forgive their sin, and will heal their land.
2 CHRONICLES 7:14

Ask, and it shall be given you; seek, and ye shall find; knock, and it shall be opened unto you.
MATTHEW 7:7

I will therefore that men pray every where, lifting up holy hands, without wrath and doubting.
1 TIMOTHY 2:8

CHAPTER FOUR

RIGHTEOUSNESS AND FAVOR

For you bless the righteous, O Lord; you cover
him with favor as with a shield.

—PSALM 5:12 ESV

IN 2010 I TRAVELED TO JERUSALEM in search of a structure to house a long-dreamed-of project—that of a museum to honor the men and women of history who worked so diligently to save the lives of Jewish men, women, and children. It would honor those Gentiles who, in some instances, put their lives on the line in order to protect Jews during the Holocaust, or fought side by side for the rebirth of the land of Israel. During that trip, I met the owners of a five-story edifice at 22 Rivlin Street, just a stone's throw from the Temple Mount. God granted me favor with them, for as we negotiated the price for the building, the owners not only lowered the price by $2 million but carried the note interest-free to the end of 2014.

In Romans 14:17–18 (NIV), Paul wrote:

For the kingdom of God is not a matter of eating and drinking, but of righteousness, peace and joy in the Holy Spirit, because anyone who serves Christ in this way is pleasing to God and receives human approval.

The key to gaining favor with man is to simply focus on delighting in the Lord; He will give you the desire of your heart (see Psalm 37:4) as well as favor when and where needed. Is that being egotistical or self-centered? Not at all; it is simply walking in the Word. Scripture reinforces the precept that we can have favor with man and enjoy God's blessings and favor when we walk uprightly before Him.

Psalm 5:12 says:

For You, O LORD, will bless the righteous;
With favor You will surround him as with a shield.

To favor means to give extraordinary honor to someone; to shower them with bounty; to demonstrate incomparable benevolence. When the angel Gabriel appeared to Mary to announce the coming birth of the Messiah, he said to her:

Rejoice, highly favored *one*, the Lord *is* with you;
blessed *are* you among women! (Luke 1:28).

As with Mary, God pursues us with grace and encompasses us with favor. He honors us with His blessings. Simply put, one who is favored is presented with benevolence and compassion, as the apostle Paul wrote to the Ephesians, "exceedingly abundantly above all that we ask or think" (3:20).

It is important to understand that God's favor is not always showered upon His children as material gifts. More often it is in the form of spiritual blessings as our lives are lived out in His righteousness:

> My son, do not forget my law, but let your heart keep my commands; for length of days and long life and peace they will add to you. Let not mercy and truth forsake you; bind them around your neck, write them on the tablet of your heart, and so find favor and high esteem in the sight of God and man (Proverbs 3:1–4).

For whoever finds me finds life, ad obtains favor from the LORD (Proverbs 8:35).

> He who earnestly seeks good finds favor
> (Proverbs 11:27).

> A good man obtains favor from the LORD
> (Proverbs 12:2).

> For You, O LORD, will bless the righteous; with favor You will surround him as with a shield (Psalm 5:12).

And one more promise from Psalm 41:11 (KJV):

> By this I know that thou favourest me, because mine enemy doth not triumph over me.

Just as both the child Samuel and our Lord grew in favor with God and man, so can you and I find favor as we live righteously before our heavenly Father. But please do not think this is some secret formula for receiving your every wish and desire from God; it is not. Remember Job. In Chapter 1, verse 8, Jehovah says to Satan:

> Have you considered My servant Job, that there is none like him on the earth, a blameless and upright man, one who fears God and shuns evil?

Even as Job was tested through tragic loss and critical analysis by his closest "comforters," he steadfastly held on to God as his strength and firm foundation. In chapter 23, verse 10, Job avers, "But He knows the way that I take; *when* He has tested me, I shall come forth as gold."

If you have studied the Bible, you know the story of Jacob—how he and his mother, Rebekah, deceived his twin brother, Esau; how he was sent away to live with his mother's brother, Laban. Soon after his arrival in Haran, Jacob fell deeply in love with his cousin Rachel. After pledging to work seven years for her hand in marriage, Jacob was deceived by Laban, who replaced Rachel at the marriage ceremony with her veiled older sister Leah. A devastated and disappointed Jacob promised to work an additional seven years in order to marry Rachel.

Although Jacob had played a role in deceiving his nearly blind father, he was still a descendant of a line of godly men, Abraham and Isaac—righteous men of honesty and principle. After Jacob had spent a week's honeymoon with Leah, Laban allowed him to marry Rachel and then serve his seven-year commitment. In seven days, Jacob went from being an enthralled young man enraptured by his beautiful younger cousin to being an overworked, underpaid husband of not one but two wives.

Over the ensuing seven years, Jehovah blessed Jacob with eleven sons and one lone daughter. Laban, too, received the blessings of God and became a very wealthy man because of his son-in-law's integrity and righteousness. At any time, Jacob could have stealthily gathered Rachel and her two sons, abandoned the covenant he had made based on Laban's deception with Leah, and could have run from his father-in-law's demands. Instead Jacob chose the way of integrity. Proverbs 11:3 says, "The integrity of the upright will guide them."

Jacob had made his peace with Jehovah, learned a very valuable lesson about deception, and had determined to live a righteous life. He served with honor for seventeen long years before asking Laban to release him and allow him to return home. Knowing that he was reaping the benefits of a righteous relative without having to pay for Jehovah's favor:

> Laban said to him, "Please stay, if I have found favor in your eyes, for I have learned by experience that the LORD has blessed me for your sake." Then he said, "Name me your wages, and I will give it" (Genesis 30:27–28).

As a result of the agreement, Jacob became a very wealthy man despite Laban's repeated attempts to cheat him. (See Genesis 30:9–43.) Perhaps it was this story of his ancestors that caused Solomon to write in Proverbs 20:7: "The righteous man walks in his integrity; his children are blessed after him."

Because of his uprightness, Jacob left the home of his father-in-law, not only with his wives and children but with God-given favor with man. That favor would extend to his first meeting with his brother, Esau, since leaving home in disgrace (see Genesis 32). Jacob would again reap favor with man because of his dedication to Jehovah God.

That is precisely how God works—what Satan means for evil, God turns to good. (See Genesis 50:20.) Pastor and author Max Lucado writes:

> God, the Master Weaver. He stretches the yarn and intertwines the colors, the ragged twine with the velvet strings, the pains with the pleasures. Nothing escapes his reach. Every king, despot, weather pattern, and molecule are at his command. He passes the shuttle back and forth across the generations, and as he does, a design emerges. Satan weaves; God reweaves.[10]

Never underestimate God's abundant blessings and man's favor bestowed on those who continue to live a righteousness life.

—DISCUSSION—
MATERIAL

1. The key to gaining favor with man is to simply focus on delighting in the Lord; He will give you the desires of your heart as well as favor when and where needed. Is that being egotistical or self-centered?

2. Does God always shower His children with material gifts?

3. What are some of the other ways God blesses us with favor with man?

4. Consider the life of Jacob and the ways God gave him favor with man.

5. How are righteousness and favor related?

—SCRIPTURES ON—
RIGHTEOUSNESS

If ye know that he is righteous, ye know that every one that doeth righteousness is born of him.
1 JOHN 2:29

Blessed are they that keep judgment, and he that doeth righteousness at all times.
PSALM 106:3

But and if ye suffer for righteousness' sake, happy are ye: and be not afraid of their terror, neither be troubled.
1 PETER 3:14

And he shall sit as a refiner and purifier of silver: and he shall purify the sons of Levi, and purge them as gold and silver, that they may offer unto the LORD an offering in righteousness.
MALACHI 3:3

Little children, let no man deceive you: he that doeth righteousness is righteous, even as he is righteous.
1 JOHN 3:7

Being filled with the fruits of righteousness, which are by Jesus Christ, unto the glory and praise of God.
PHILIPPIANS 1:11

For I say unto you, That except your righteousness shall exceed the righteousness of the scribes and Pharisees, ye shall in no case enter into the kingdom of heaven.
MATTHEW 5:20

And he believed in the LORD; and he counted it to him for righteousness.

GENESIS 15:6

Simon Peter, a servant and an apostle of Jesus Christ, to them that have obtained like precious faith with us through the righteousness of God and our Saviour Jesus Christ.

2 PETER 1:1

Teaching us that, denying ungodliness and worldly lusts, we should live soberly, righteously, and godly, in this present world.

TITUS 2:12

Flee also youthful lusts: but follow righteousness, faith, charity, peace, with them that call on the Lord out of a pure heart.

2 TIMOTHY 2:22

Now he that ministereth seed to the sower both minister bread for your food, and multiply your seed sown, and increase the fruits of your righteousness.

2 CORINTHIANS 9:10

But of him are ye in Christ Jesus, who of God is made unto us wisdom, and righteousness, and sanctification, and redemption.

1 CORINTHIANS 1:30

That as sin hath reigned unto death, even so might grace reign through righteousness unto eternal life by Jesus Christ our Lord.

ROMANS 5:21

CHAPTER FIVE

THE TRUTH OF THE WORD YIELDS FAVOR

The righteous cry out, and the LORD hears,
And delivers them out of all their troubles.

—PSALM 34:17

SOME YEARS AGO, I awakened early in my hotel room in Orlando, Florida, to catch a flight to Michigan. As soon as I got settled on the plane, I fell asleep. Hours later, in a daze, I heard the pilot announcing, "We're now over Phoenix, Arizona." I was totally confused. I asked the attendant, "How can we possibly be over Phoenix? We're going to Michigan."

"This plane is not bound for Michigan," she replied. "We are on our way to Los Angeles."

My first reaction was frustration; then I heard the Holy Spirit whisper, *"Pray."* As I obeyed, He said I was going as a witness for Him during this unplanned detour. After we landed at the Los Angeles airport, I tried to be sensitive to the direction of the Spirit, but didn't detect the urge to witness to anyone. Frustrated again and berating myself for being so foolish as to board the wrong flight, I found a seat to wait for the only departure that would take me back in the direction of Michigan—a flight to Ohio.

By the time I boarded the plane, I was so distressed I did the very thing that had gotten me into that mess in the first place. Ignoring the man sitting beside me, I grabbed a pillow and settled in for a nap. Unfortunately for me, he wanted to talk. Finally, unable to sleep, I opened my eyes and looked at him. "You must be somebody," he grinned.

Not sure why he thought that, I responded, "A somebody who thinks he's somebody is nobody, but a nobody who experiences Somebody becomes somebody. As long as somebody thinks he's somebody, he will always be nobody."

The man looked dumbfounded. "What are you talking about?"

At that instant, Jesus whispered, *"This is the man."*

As we talked, the Holy Spirit gave me insight about his life, a word regarding a past divorce and devastating personal problems. It was as though I had opened his personal diary.

The color drained from his face as he demanded, "Who are you? You are frightening me." He thought I was a federal agent who had been planted to confront him. Over the course of the next couple of hours, I was able to pray with him and lead him to the Lord. God had used what I—and others—may have thought was a crazy situation to deliver a message of salvation.

Jehovah used an equally unusual circumstance to afford David the opportunity to preach to Achish (sometimes referred to as Abimelech), king of Gath in 1 Samuel 21:10–15:

> [David] went to Achish, king of Gath. When the
> servants of Achish saw him, they said, "Can this be

David, the famous David? Is this the one they sing of at their dances? Saul kills by the thousand, David by the ten thousand!" When David realized that he had been recognized, he panicked, fearing the worst from Achish, king of Gath. So right there, while they were looking at him, he pretended to go crazy, pounding his head on the city gate and foaming at the mouth, spit dripping from his beard. Achish took one look at him and said to his servants, "Can't you see he's crazy? Why did you let him in here? Don't you think I have enough crazy people to put up with as it is without adding another? Get him out of here!" (MSG)

What benefit could possibly have been achieved by David pretending to be insane, other than the obvious one—to preserve his life and the lives of his followers? It is entirely feasible that God had tapped His servant David to present a message to the king that would, under different circumstances, have meant the death of the messenger. When David wrote Psalm 34 it was assigned the heading, "When he pretended to be insane before Abimelech."

Achish used the word *mad* three times as he derided his soldiers for bringing into his presence the man who had killed Goliath, Gath's finest. Initially, the words were used to describe "one who has sudden, unpredictable, wild outbursts of uncontrollable anger for no apparent reason." Or, in Achish's mind, it was the perfect picture of the man standing before him. Can you see David—slobbering, banging his head against the doorposts, wild-eyed (likely with fear at the situation in which he now found himself), and pacing with agitation? Perhaps Achish was afraid of the future king of Judah, although by then David had been completely mortified and disgraced. Achish then ordered his soldiers to unceremoniously dump David outside the gates of the city.

Did David begin to sing this song before the pagan king as he was being dragged away? Allow me to paraphrase Psalm 34, if you will:

O King, Achish, you can belittle me and ridicule my God, but

I will bless the Lord at all times: His praise shall continually be in my mouth.

You may boast of your manmade gods and idols, but

My soul shall make its boast in the Lord; the humble shall hear of it and be glad.

Instead of praising gods who have no power:

Oh, magnify the Lord with me, and let us exalt His name together.

Of course, my men and I were afraid when I was led into this room, but

I sought the Lord, and He heard me, and delivered me from all my fears. They looked to Him and were radiant, and their faces were not ashamed. This poor man cried out, and the Lord heard him, and saved him out of all his troubles.

O King, Achish, can you not see for yourself? Hovering up there in the corner of the room, standing there behind your rank of soldiers, surrounding me and my men:

The angel of the Lord encamps all around those who fear Him, and delivers them.

King, you just simply don't know what you are missing:

Oh, taste and see that the Lord is good; blessed is the man who trusts in Him!

Rev. Bill Versteeg wrote of David's song:

To the Philistine, humans were around to serve the gods, keep the gods happy so that they might get some return in prosperity and fertility. Before the gods, human lives were nothing—sacrificeable just to keep the gods satisfied. But David says *Taste and see that the LORD is good;*—as if God is someone to be enjoyed, cherished, loved. As if God is like the best of wines, the choicest of foods, the most fulfilling of choices, the most rewarding relationship, a love that is better than life. God serving us—to the point that he watches us and waits for us to call to him . . . . *The eyes of the LORD are on the righteous and his ears are attentive to their cry;* Such irreverence would not be tolerated—except that it looked profoundly insane.[11]

Perhaps those in the assembly looked at each other and asked, "Is this the same man who slew the giant of Gath? He has totally lost it! Maybe the resounding thud of Goliath hitting the rocky ground rattled David's brain. It is a good thing, for otherwise Achish would have this foolish man's head on a spike by the front gate for all the country to see."

Every word David delivered before the court of the king of Gath was the absolute truth. He challenged the Philistine hoards with the oracles of Jehovah God and then preserved it for all eternity as a song of God's faithfulness to His children. It could be that the prophet Hosea was remembering this psalm of David's all those years later when he wrote:

> Because your sins ARE so many and your hostility so great, the prophet is considered a fool, the inspired person a maniac (Hosea 9:7 NIV).

The apostle Paul wrote:

> Instead, God chose things the world considers foolish in order to shame those who think they are wise. And he chose things that are powerless to shame those who are powerful (1 Corinthians 1:27 NLT).

The fundamental answer to finding favor with man is making Jehovah God our priority:

> But seek first the kingdom of God and His righteousness, and all these things shall be added to you (Matthew 6:33).

When our sole purpose, ambition, and objective is to please our heavenly Father, we reap the benefit of finding favor with Him—and as a divine dividend we find that we are blessed with favor from man.

—DISCUSSION—
MATERIAL

1. Read the story of David found in 1 Samuel 21.

2. What benefit could possibly have been achieved by David pretending to be insane, other than the obvious one—to preserve his life and the lives of his followers?

3. Has God ever prompted you to do something that was out of your comfort zone?

4. Read Matthew 6:33. Why is this passage of Scripture the fundamental answer to finding favor with God and man?

5. Recall an experience when you were able to share the Word with someone because of God-given favor with man.

— S C R I P T U R E S   O N —
THE WORD OF GOD

For the word of God is quick, and powerful, and sharper than any twoedged sword, piercing even to the dividing asunder of soul and spirit, and of the joints and marrow, and is a discerner of the thoughts and intents of the heart.
HEBREWS 4:12

All scripture is given by inspiration of God, and is profitable for doctrine, for reproof, for correction, for instruction in righteousness.
2 TIMOTHY 3:16

Is not my word like as a fire? saith the LORD; and like a hammer that breaketh the rock in pieces?
JEREMIAH 23:29

Thy word is a lamp unto my feet, and a light unto my path.
PSALM 119:105

And they overcame him by the blood of the Lamb, and by the word of their testimony; and they loved not their lives unto the death.
REVELATION 12:11

That which was from the beginning, which we have heard, which we have seen with our eyes, which we have looked upon, and our hands have handled, of the Word of life.
1 JOHN 1:1

Who his own self bare our sins in his own body on the tree, that we, being dead to sins, should live unto righteousness: by whose stripes ye were healed.
1 PETER 2:24

And take the helmet of salvation, and the sword of the Spirit, which is the word of God.
EPHESIANS 6:17

So then faith cometh by hearing, and hearing by the word of God.
ROMANS 10:17

Sanctify them through thy truth: thy word is truth.
JOHN 17:17

But he answered and said, It is written, Man shall not live by bread alone, but by every word that proceedeth out of the mouth of God.
MATTHEW 4:4

So shall my word be that goeth forth out of my mouth: it shall not return unto me void, but it shall accomplish that which I please, and it shall prosper in the thing whereto I sent it.
ISAIAH 55:11

The grass withereth, the flower fadeth: but the word of our God shall stand for ever.
ISAIAH 40:8

In the beginning was the Word, and the Word was with God, and the Word was God.
JOHN 1:1-2

CHAPTER SIX

SUBMISSION
SECURES FAVOR

For You have made him a little lower than the angels,
And You have crowned him with glory and honor.

—PSALM 8:5

MY EARLY DAYS AS A CHRISTIAN brought me face-to-face with a scripture I would have been just as happy to exclude from my Bible. It is found in Exodus right in the middle of the Ten Commandments: "Honor your father and your mother . . . " Honoring my mother was not a difficult task, but honoring my abusive father was on the "impossible" scale. If you know my story, you are aware that I was physically and emotionally abused from an early age, and almost strangled to death by my anti-Semitic father. So you might imagine my chagrin when I discerned that the Holy Spirit was leading me to apologize to Dad.

I knew he still had power over me but, for some reason I failed to understand, his acceptance was still of paramount importance to me. Dad had to know that Jesus was real in my life. I wanted him to see that a true encounter with God could change his life forever, and

I wanted to be free from the spider web in which he had entangled me.

After traveling to his home and greeting him, I obeyed what I knew to be God's leading. I got on my knees and said, "Dad, God wants me to humble myself and ask your forgiveness for any sins I've committed against you." I began to confess my failures as a son—pride, not praying for him as I should, and others. I didn't enumerate his wrongs against me. I didn't recount the beatings at his hands or the curses from his mouth. He was horrified and ordered me to stop, but I continued on.

Suddenly he cried, "Stop it! I can't take any more. I have committed the unpardonable sin for what I have done to you. I can never be saved! My home will be eternal hell."

As I talked to Dad about Jesus and what He meant in my life, his hard exterior began to crack. Then he leaned forward in his seat and gripped my hands so hard his knuckles turned white. "Son," he cried, "I should have been put in prison for what I done to you."

I felt his tears running down my neck as he began to weep. God's grace and mercy captivated me. I found my heart overflowing with compassion for the man I thought I could never forgive, much less love, and I led him to a real relationship with Christ there in his living room. My submission to the directive of the Holy Spirit was the beginning of a healing process that lasted until the day he died.

By that time in my ministry, I had learned about the role of favor in the life of a Believer—favor with God and with man—but over nearly sixty years of walking with my heavenly Father, I have learned what a valuable role submission plays in receiving that reward. I know that the grace of God will bring supernatural favor with man. There is a definite demarcation between ordinary and extraordinary favor—one can be achieved by hard work and charm;

the other is an unearned gift from Jehovah-Jireh, my supernatural Provider.

Being naturally favored is hard work! It is a struggle to say and do the right thing, flatter the right people, kowtow to those in power, bow and scrape at the exact moment—and of course, smile through it all. Don't misunderstand; being kind is always the proper motive for anything we do as Believers. But supernatural favor is a gift from our loving and gracious Father. He simply wants us to be submissive to His will no matter how difficult that might be. And I can tell you it wasn't easy to surrender my will and humble myself before my earthly father to ask his forgiveness. At times, the words stuck in my throat, but I just had to follow God's direction and leave the rest to Him.

Our perfect example is Jesus who "humbled Himself and became obedient to *the point of* death, even the death of the cross" (Philippians 2:8). Our Lord had walked in favor with God and man, but especially throughout His three years of ministry. Even those who were sent to arrest Him recognized that special something that permeated the very atmosphere around Jesus. They returned to the High Priest who had dispatched them and reported, "No man ever spoke like this Man!" (See John 7:46.)

What many miss about gaining supernatural favor through surrender to God's perfect will is that we must be "partakers of [His] divine nature." (See 2 Peter 1:4.) And we must avail ourselves of what our Father has offered. How do we do that? We must face every situation with the confidence that "if God is for us, who can be against us?" (See Romans 8:31.)

There are numerous examples in the pages of Scripture of men and women who began life in obscurity and were raised up into positions of prominence—David, Ruth, Esther, Joseph, and Gideon.

These individuals received supernatural favor from kings, priests, generals, and wealthy landowners. Because of their submission to the will and plan of God for their lives, David became a king, Esther a queen, Joseph a leader over all Egypt, Ruth an ancestor of our Lord, and Gideon a mighty warrior. Each overcame vastly different circumstances to enjoy the favor of man.

Rev. Paul Aiello Jr. shared an illustration about submission that has a valuable lesson for each of us:

> The captain of the ship looked into the dark night and saw faint lights in the distance. Immediately he told his signalman to send a message: "Alter your course 10 degrees south."
>
> Promptly a return message was received: "Alter your course 10 degrees north."
>
> The captain was angered; his command had been ignored. So he sent a second message: "Alter your course 10 degrees south—I am the captain!"
>
> Soon another message was received: "Alter your course 10 degrees north—I am seaman third class Jones."
>
> Immediately the captain sent a third message, knowing the fear it would evoke: "Alter your course 10 degrees south—I am a battleship."
>
> Then the reply came: "Alter your course 10 degrees north—I am a lighthouse."[12]

In the midst of our dark and foggy times, all sorts of voices are shouting orders into the night, telling us what to do, how to adjust our lives. Out of the darkness, one voice signals something quite opposite to the rest—something almost absurd. But the voice happens to be the Light of the World, and we ignore it at our peril.

When we submit to the lordship of Jesus Christ, a benefit of that surrender is favor with man. Had the captain of the ship continued on his course, the entire ship, its crew and its contents could have been lost.

Submission to the voice of the Holy Spirit saved the life of the apostle Paul and his shipboard companions while he was sailing to Rome to appeal to Caesar.

The ship's captain was determined to put out to sea despite Paul's admonition:

> Men, I perceive that this voyage will end with disaster and much loss, not only of the cargo and ship, but also our lives, (Acts 27:10).

Supported by the centurion in charge of the prisoners, it was determined that the ship could reach the next scheduled port without difficulty. Readying the ship, the crew hoisted the sails on the first sunny day and the order was given for the vessel to glide from the harbor into the choppy waters of the Mediterranean. Several hours after leaving port—at the point of no return—a storm overtook the ship. Unable to turn back to the port at Fair Havens and too far from their designated destination, the craft and its terrified crew were left to be battered by the angry waves. It would have been well within Paul's right to toss out a hearty "I told you so!" Instead, he did the one thing he knew would help the situation: He began to fast and pray.

The crew slaved to save the craft, tossing out everything that could be safely spared in an attempt to lighten the ship. And then they waited, fearing each moment might be their last as the battered vessel wallowed from wave to trough through the dark, stormy night. Hour after hour, the darkness blanketed the hopeless travelers as the storm raged.

Now it was time for Paul to remind those in charge that the warning had been given—but they were not without hope:

> "Men, you should have listened to me, and not have sailed from Crete and incurred this disaster and loss. And now I urge you to take heart, for there will be no loss of life among you, but only of the ship. For there stood by me this night an angel of the God to whom I belong and whom I serve, saying, 'Do not be afraid, Paul; you must be brought before Caesar; and indeed God has granted you all those who sail with you.' Therefore take heart, men, for I believe God that it will be just as it was told me. However, we must run aground on a certain island" (Acts 27:21–26).

Another two long weeks passed before Paul's prophecy was fulfilled and the ship was driven toward the rocky shore of the island of Melita, today known as Malta. The crew, in an attempt to halt the forward progress of the craft, threw the anchors out and prepared to lower the lifeboats to save themselves. The prisoners and passengers would either be killed by the sword or left to die in the roiling waters. Again Paul addressed the centurion with whom he had found favor and admonished, "Unless these men stay in the ship, you cannot be saved" (Acts 27:31).

The soldiers were ordered to cut the lifeboats free from their moorings and let them drop into the sea. Hours later as the ship began to break apart from the pounding waves, the centurion ordered everyone that could swim into the sea and admonished those who could not to cling to pieces of flotsam from the ship in order to reach shore. When all were gathered on the sandy beach, not a single person had been lost, just as Paul had intimated. The two hundred seventy-six passengers huddled against the cold wind. The order was given to gather wood for a fire, so the islanders who had greeted them set off to find dry kindling. Then the wet and bedraggled crew, passengers, and prisoners encircled the bonfire. As Paul gathered a bundle of sticks to feed the flames, a deadly viper hidden amidst the firewood latched on to Paul's hand.

Thinking that Paul must have been a very evil man to have been targeted by the snake, a hush fell over the noisy gathering as the inhabitants waited for him to die from the venom injected into his bloodstream. They were puzzled and stunned when Paul simply shook the viper off into the fire and went about his business. The people concluded that rather than evil, Paul must surely be a god—someone to be worshipped.

Paul's submission to Jehovah and his determination to deliver the Word he had received during the voyage gave him favor with the ruler of the island, a man named Publius. After hearing the story of the snakebite, Publius invited Paul and his friends (Luke, the physician, and Aristarchus) to his home, where he entertained them for three days. While there, Paul learned that the father of their host was sick with a fever. Not wanting to miss an opportunity to present the Good News of Jesus Christ, Paul prayed for the ill man and he was healed. As a result, many from across the island who suffered from sickness made their way to see the prisoner who had escaped the sea and the viper. Paul was able to share the gospel with those who gathered until the time came to set sail for Rome. (See Acts 28.)

Submission to the Father produces favor with man and can bring souls to the kingdom of God. Favor with man opens doors that may otherwise be closed and locked. Favor is God's will for the Believer. When God grants you favor with man, it would be wise to follow the advice of British biologist Francis Maitland Balfour, the younger brother of Lord Arthur Balfour, who said:

> The best thing to give your enemy is forgiveness; to an opponent, tolerance; to a friend, your heart; to your child, a good example; to a father, deference; to your mother, conduct that will make her proud of you; to yourself, respect; to all men, charity.[13]

Those are the keys to continued God-given favor with man.

— DISCUSSION —
MATERIAL

1. Read Acts 27, the story of Paul's shipwreck.

2. List and reflect on the various people with whom God gave him favor.

3. What do you think was the one thing that saved the lives of Paul and his shipmates?

4. Why is submission to the Holy Spirit so important in the life of a Believer?

5. Who are some of the people in your life with whom you need favor?

—SCRIPTURES ON—
SUBMISSION

Submit yourselves therefore to God. Resist the devil, and he will flee from you.
JAMES 4:7

Submitting yourselves one to another in the fear of God.
EPHESIANS 5:21

But be ye doers of the word, and not hearers only, deceiving your own selves.
JAMES 1:22

Trust in the LORD with all thine heart; and lean not unto thine own understanding.
PROVERBS 3:5

Saying with a loud voice, Fear God, and give glory to him; for the hour of his judgment is come: and worship him that made heaven, and earth, and the sea, and the fountains of waters.
REVELATION 14:7

Thou shalt not bow down thyself to them, nor serve them: for I the LORD thy God am a jealous God, visiting the iniquity of the fathers upon the children unto the third and fourth generation of them that hate me.
EXODUS 20:5

Likewise, ye younger, submit yourselves unto the elder. Yea, all of you be subject one to another, and be clothed with humility: for God resisteth the proud, and giveth grace to the humble.
1 PETER 5:5

Servants, be obedient to them that are your masters according to the flesh, with fear and trembling, in singleness of your heart, as unto Christ.
EPHESIANS 6:5

I exhort therefore, that, first of all, supplications, prayers, intercessions, and giving of thanks, be made for all men.
1 TIMOTHY 2:1

Wives, submit yourselves unto your own husbands, as unto the Lord.
EPHESIANS 5:22

Let every soul be subject unto the higher powers. For there is no power but of God: the powers that be are ordained of God.
ROMANS 13:1

But the LORD said unto Samuel, Look not on his countenance, or on the height of his stature; because I have refused him: for theLORD seeth not as man seeth; for man looketh on the outward appearance, but the LORD looketh on the heart.
1 SAMUEL 16:7

Submit yourselves to every ordinance of man for the Lord's sake: whether it be to the king, as supreme.
1 PETER 2:13

Remember them which have the rule over you, who have spoken unto you the word of God: whose faith follow, considering the end of their conversation.
HEBREWS 13:7

CHAPTER SEVEN

GENEROSITY
GRANTS FAVOR

*"Give, and it will be given to you: good measure, pressed down,
shaken together, and running over will be put into your bosom.
For with the same measure that you use, it
will be measured back to you."*

—LUKE 6:38

AS WORK PROGRESSED on the Friends of Zion Heritage
Center (FOZHC) in Jerusalem, the team involved with the project determined that more space was needed to accommodate tour
groups waiting to see the museum. Where that space could be
found was a challenge. Behind the five-story building that houses
FOZHC is a coffee shop that would be perfect for such use, but
the owners had no desire to sell or lease the building. We needed
miraculous favor with man in order to fulfill the need.

In its former life, the museum building had been a school complete with dorm rooms for students. Once the conversion began,
it was determined that the furnishings would have to be sold or
donated to empty the rooms. The decision was made to donate the

beds, dressers, and other items to an organization that aided elderly Holocaust survivors in Israel.

The day came when a truck backed up to the door of the building and workers began to load the furnishings. One of the owners of the coffee shop saw the activity and asked what would happen to the fixtures. When he was told that they would be donated to Holocaust survivors, he was incredulous. We assured him that this was, indeed, true. It was the key to opening the door that eventually led to FOZHC being allowed to purchase the building. The generosity of the Friends of Zion team led to the miracle of favor with man that was so needed to complete the multimillion-dollar project.

King David exhibited one of the most loving acts of generosity shown in the pages of Scripture. The story of the shepherd boy who slew a giant and became king is well-known. Also often told is David's daily battle to outwit a crazed King Saul and escape his rabid determination to kill the future king of Judah. David vehemently refused to touch the man God had chosen to be anointed as king.

Finally Saul met his match when faced with the army of the Philistines at Mount Gilboa, where he was severely wounded by enemy archers. Rather than face capture and certain death at the hands of a pagan king, Saul fell on his own sword to escape such ignominy. Three of his sons also fell during the battle, including Jonathan, David's beloved friend.

After David ascended the throne, he could easily have followed the example of other kings and hunted down his predecessor's male relatives to prevent attempts to regain control of the throne. This king after God's own heart (see 1 Samuel 13:14) chose instead to offer kindness and consideration because he had made a covenant with Jonathan:

"But you shall not cut off your kindness from my house forever, no, not when the LORD has cut off every one of the enemies of David from the face of the earth." So Jonathan made *a covenant* with the house of David, *saying,* "Let the LORD require *it* at the hand of David's enemies" (1 Samuel 20:15–16).

Intending to honor his promise to his friend, David called in one of his servants and asked, "Is there still anyone who is left of the house of Saul, that I may show him kindness for Jonathan's sake?" (See 2 Samuel 9:1.) Kindness can sometimes be misconstrued as weakness rather than a profound act of love—one that is unmerited and cannot be repaid.

The hunt was on; David dispatched servants to track down any remaining relatives of King Saul. That may not have been an easy task, as fear would have kept them in hiding. Finally, Jonathan's crippled son (see 2 Samuel 4:4), Mephibosheth, was located—living in abject poverty and anonymity in a far-flung and desolate corner of the land.

Mephibosheth was summoned to the palace, where he shuffled into the presence of the most powerful man in the kingdom—King David. What were his expectations? I believe he anticipated the worst and expected to hear, "Off with his head!" Proverbs 23:7 warns, "For as he thinks in his heart, so *is* he." In his heart, Mephibosheth saw himself as worthless, polluted by his association with King Saul. Perhaps Mephibosheth imagined the feel of a cold blade against the back of his neck as he fell on his face before the king.

As with this sad young man, if we as Believers expect to grow in favor with God and with man, our level of expectation must be raised; not in a sense of arrogance, but based on Scripture. This is what we should expect that favor to look like:

> Bless the LORD, O my soul,
> And forget not all His benefits:
> Who forgives all your iniquities,
> Who heals all your diseases,
> Who redeems your life from destruction,
> Who crowns you with lovingkindness and tender mercies,
> Who satisfies your mouth with good things,
> So that your youth is renewed like the eagle's . . . .
> But the mercy of the LORD *is* from everlasting to everlasting
> On those who fear Him,
> And His righteousness to children's children,
> To such as keep His covenant,
> And to those who remember His commandments to do them (Psalm 103:2–5, 17–18).

Imagine Mephibosheth's shock when he heard:

> Fear not: for I will surely shew thee kindness for Jonathan thy father's sake, and will restore thee all the land of Saul thy father; and thou shalt eat bread at my table continually (2 Samuel 9:7 KJV).

What an act of generosity! Because David had found favor with men in his life, he was unafraid to extend that same favor to others. He reached out in love and generosity to show the kindness that

Mephibosheth had never experienced. David had extended grace to the son of his friend. Given his living conditions and his handicap, it may well have been years since this outcast had heard words of compassion and consideration.

In 2 Samuel 9:8 (NLT), Jonathan's son responded much as we might have:

> Mephibosheth bowed respectfully and exclaimed, "Who is your servant, that you should show such kindness to a dead dog like me?"

In today's vernacular, he might have asked, "Why me, Lord?" Have you ever asked that question when faced with life's challenges; when the loss of a job, fear, abandonment, illness, divorce, a shattered relationship plagues you? God responds to us, "I want to open the windows of heaven and pour you out a blessing that you cannot contain (see Malachi 3:10). I want you to walk in My favor."

Words can be powerful, curative, and restorative. I am reminded of my own story and the first time I heard the word *"son"* gently spoken. Just as the soft voice of Jesus changed my life, the sympathetic voice of David changed the life of Mephibosheth. Proverbs 25:11 tells us, "A word fitly spoken *is like* apples of gold in settings of silver"—things of beauty. The child's verse, "Sticks and stones may break my bones, but words will never harm me," is wholly inaccurate: Words *can* destroy.

Mephibosheth's life had likely been one of hurtful words hurled at breakneck speed, penetrating his very soul. Now, in one grand and life-changing act of kindness, this long-forgotten grandson of a king had been restored. He was granted a perpetual pension; he became family, wrapped in the serenity of knowing someone cared.

He moved from the desert to the dining room of the king, from a dwelling of desolation to a palace of plenty, from abandoned to adopted. For years he had lived as nobody; now he was somebody—he mattered. God had blessed Mephibosheth with the favor of not just any man, but that of a king.

Teacher and author Chuck Swindoll wrote of Mephibosheth's blessing at the hand of King David:

> They talked together and laughed together and ate delicious meals together because he was a member of the family . . . and the tablecloth covered his crippled feet. Moments like that remind us that God will look at His children and say . . . "You're in My family. You're as important to Me as all my other sons and daughters." It will take eternity for us to adequately express what this truth means to us—that He chose us in our sinful and rebellious condition and in grace took us from a barren place and gave us a place at His table. And, in love, allowed His tablecloth of grace to cover our sin. Grace. It really is *amazing!*[14]

The subject of favor has a tendency to become very divisive in the Church. As journalist John Eckhardt wrote:

> We want to be blessed and live the abundant life Christ died to give us, yet we don't want to approach God as if He is a lottery or a slot machine—if you put in the right amount of prayer, praise, worship, faith and good works, out comes your blessing.[15]

Such divine favor is not simply monetary in nature. While Mephibosheth did receive financial restoration, he was also given life and the promise of peace. He would reside under the banner and sponsorship of King David. His every need would be met as he dined at the king's table—not as a beggar, not as a guest, but as a son. He would be the recipient of great favor and grace.

Remember the story of the prodigal son who awoke from his rebellion with the certain knowledge that his father's house offered peace and safety—even for the servants. So he arose and made his way home. But then his father, who had for years, perhaps, looked longingly over the landscape for a glimpse of his wayward child, caught sight of the lost son. The father ran to embrace his offspring and celebrated his return—not as a servant, but as a son! Such was Mephibosheth's welcome—that of a beloved son. I can imagine his wonder as David presented him with new clothes to replace the homespun garments of yesterday, and with jewels befitting the favored son of a king.

—DISCUSSION—
MATERIAL

1. Read 2 Samuel 9.

2. What prompted David to begin a nationwide search for Mephibosheth?

3. What do you think might have been Mephibosheth's reaction to David's generosity?

4. Have you ever been generously blessed by someone? What was your response?

5. Has God ever asked you to give generously to someone? How did you respond?

—SCRIPTURES ON—
GENEROSITY

I have shewed you all things, how that so labouring ye ought to support the weak, and to remember the words of the Lord Jesus, how he said, It is more blessed to give than to receive.

ACTS 20:35

Give, and it shall be given unto you; good measure, pressed down, and shaken together, and running over, shall men give into your bosom. For with the same measure that ye mete withal it shall be measured to you again.

LUKE 6:38

And whosoever shall give to drink unto one of these little ones a cup of cold water only in the name of a disciple, verily I say unto you, he shall in no wise lose his reward.

MATTHEW 10:42

For where your treasure is, there will your heart be also.

MATTHEW 6:21

But whoso hath this world's good, and seeth his brother have need, and shutteth up his bowels of compassion from him, how dwelleth the love of God in him?

1 JOHN 3:17

But this I say, He which soweth sparingly shall reap also sparingly; and he which soweth bountifully shall reap also bountifully.

2 CORINTHIANS 9:6

Whoso stoppeth his ears at the cry of the poor, he also shall cry himself, but shall not be heard.

PROVERBS 21:13

Therefore I thought it necessary to exhort the brethren, that they would go before unto you, and make up beforehand your bounty, whereof ye had notice before, that the same might be ready, as a matter of bounty, and not as of covetousness.

2 CORINTHIANS 9:5–7

Sell that ye have, and give alms; provide yourselves bags which wax not old, a treasure in the heavens that faileth not, where no thief approacheth, neither moth corrupteth.

LUKE 12:33

And sold their possessions and goods, and parted them to all men, as every man had need.

ACTS 2:45

His lord said unto him, Well done, thou good and faithful servant: thou hast been faithful over a few things, I will make thee ruler over many things: enter thou into the joy of thy lord.

MATTHEW 25:21

Take heed that ye do not your alms before men, to be seen of them: otherwise ye have no reward of your Father which is in heaven.

MATTHEW 6:1

If there be among you a poor man of one of thy brethren within any of thy gates in thy land which the LORD thy God giveth thee, thou shalt not harden thine heart, nor shut thine hand from thy poor brother.

DEUTERONOMY 15:7

CHAPTER EIGHT

THE BLESSINGS
OF FAVOR

*Speak now in the hearing of the people, and let every man ask from his
neighbor and every woman from her neighbor, articles of silver and
articles of gold." And the LORD gave the people favor in the sight of
the Egyptians. Moreover the man Moses was very great in the land of
Egypt, in the sight of Pharaoh's servants and in the sight of the people.*

—EXODUS 11:2-3

EXODUS, THE SECOND BOOK of the Pentateuch, is the story
of deliverance from bondage and restoration—the establishing of
a special relationship between Jehovah and the children of Israel.

Chapter one relates that after having enjoyed life in Egypt under
the umbrella of Joseph, who had been named lord of Pharoah's
house, the time came when a new Pharaoh ascended the throne.
The new ruler had never heard of Joseph or of the Israelite's heroic
efforts during the seven years of drought that devastated the land.
The demon of jealousy gripped Pharaoh:

> And he said to his people, "Look, the people of
> the children of Israel are more and mightier than
> we; come, let us deal shrewdly with them, lest they

multiply, and it happen, in the event of war, that they also join our enemies and fight against us, and so go up out of the land." Therefore they set taskmasters over them to afflict them with their burdens (Exodus 1:9–11).

During the ensuing 430 years, the offspring of Jacob lived under Egyptian bondage, which grew exponentially as the Israelites continued to multiply. Meanwhile Moses was living on the backside of the desert, working as a shepherd for his father-in-law, Jethro. For forty long years, the man who was to deliver God's people from bondage wandered the arid landscape, herding sheep. He was charged with keeping them safe, tending their wounds, finding food and water, securing shelter, and identifying the predators that could decimate the herd in a matter of minutes.

God was hardening Moses to desert life in the place he would spend another forty years of his life. The adopted son of Pharaoh's daughter was learning meekness and humility and, at the same time, growing physically stronger and more hardened for the task ahead. At the end of forty years, Moses would be charged with stalking into the throne room of the most powerful man in the region and demanding that he allow the Israelites—his bond slaves—to pack up and leave Goshen. Moses was about to transition from being nobody to being somebody. He was about to receive enormous preference from the Egyptians because of God's grace and favor.

After Moses encountered his blood brother, Aaron, in the desert, the two men made their way to the palace to challenge Pharaoh. With his refusal to let the Israelites go, God began to visit ten plagues on the land. Rather than persuade the ruler, it did the opposite and the burdens that had been placed on the children of Jacob were intensified.

The last plague, the death of all of Egypt's firstborn, was the final straw for the rebellious Pharaoh. Beginning in Exodus 11:4 Moses and Aaron were sent to warn the Egyptian ruler of what was to come:

> "Thus says the LORD: 'About midnight I will go out into the midst of Egypt; and all the firstborn in the land of Egypt shall die, from the firstborn of Pharaoh who sits on his throne, even to the firstborn of the female servant who is behind the handmill, and all the firstborn of the animals. Then there shall be a great cry throughout all the land of Egypt, such as was not like it before, nor shall be like it again. But against none of the children of Israel shall a dog move its tongue, against man or beast, that you may know that the LORD does make a difference between the Egyptians and Israel.' And all these your servants shall come down to me and bow down to me, saying, 'Get out, and all the people who follow you!' After that I will go out." Then he went out from Pharaoh in great anger.

Moses was vitally aware of what was about to befall the Egyptian people. Remember, as a baby he was saved by Pharaoh's daughter because of an edict that demanded the deaths of all babies born to the children of Israel. The king's disobedience would exact a dire penalty, not only on his household but also of each one in the land of Egypt. Harsh, yes, but Pharaoh had been given numerous opportunities to heed the voice of Jehovah. Because He is a God of love, He made a way for the Israelites to escape the sentence of death that had been pronounced. Jehovah-Jireh, my Provider, offered safety to those who would listen and obey His commands.

The night before the Passover lamb was to be offered and its blood applied to the doorposts of the homes of every Israelite, Jehovah sent them forth to their neighbors and gave them great favor and specific instructions:

> And the LORD said to Moses, "I will bring one more plague on Pharaoh and on Egypt. Afterward he will let you go from here. When he lets you go, he will surely drive you out of here altogether. Speak now in the hearing of the people, and let every man ask from his neighbor and every woman from her neighbor, articles of silver and articles of gold." And the LORD gave the people favor in the sight of the Egyptians. Moreover the man Moses was very great in the land of Egypt, in the sight of Pharaoh's servants and in the sight of the people (Exodus 11:1–3).

What incredible favor extended to a group of slaves! What would your reaction be if someone knocked on your door and politely asked you for your gold and silver—assuming you had any? God had paved the way for His people. When the knock sounded on the door, whatever was owned by the Egyptian captors was readily given to the Israelites. In Exodus 3:21–22, we see another description of this event:

> And I will give this people favor in the sight of the Egyptians; and it shall be, when you go, that you shall not go empty-handed. But every woman shall ask of her neighbor, namely, of her who dwells near her house, articles of silver, articles of gold, and clothing; and you shall put them on your sons and on your daughters. So you shall plunder the Egyptians.

Joseph's ancestors were set free bearing the blessings of Jehovah as they hurriedly followed Moses to the Red Sea. Psalm 105:37 says, "He also brought them out with *silver and gold,* and there was *none feeble* among his tribes." In the midst of their captivity, Jehovah-Mephalti—the Lord my Deliverer—blessed His people with both health and wealth.

Moses discovered that the favor of Jehovah God could open doors that no man could shut! It provided material goods that would never have been offered to the suffering Israelites in bondage to the Egyptians. Can you picture those who opened their doors to the knocking of their Hebrew neighbors, bowing and hurrying back inside to fulfill the requests of their hated and feared enemies? God's blessings produced favor with man for the children of Israel—and it will for you.

Was this abundance of wealth simply to line the pockets of the Israelites—to pay them back for all the years of hard labor under the harsh reign of Pharaoh? No, it was for a greater purpose: God would ask that His people open their hearts and coffers to provide the materials needed to build the tabernacle:

> Then everyone came whose heart was stirred, and everyone whose spirit was willing, and they brought the LORD's offering for the work of the tabernacle of meeting, for all its service, and for the holy garments. They came, both men and women, as many as had a willing heart, and brought earrings and nose rings, rings and necklaces, all jewelry of gold, that is, every man who made an offering of gold to the LORD. And every man, with whom was found blue, purple, and scarlet thread, fine linen, and goats' hair, red skins of

rams, and badger skins, brought them. Everyone who offered an offering of silver or bronze brought the LORD's offering. And everyone with whom was found acacia wood for any work of the service, brought it . . . . The rulers brought onyx stones, and the stones to be set in the ephod and in the breastplate, and spices and oil for the light, for the anointing oil, and for the sweet incense. The children of Israel brought a freewill offering to the LORD, all the men and women whose hearts were willing to bring material for all kinds of work which the LORD, by the hand of Moses, had commanded to be done (Exodus 35:21–24, 27–29).

God had granted favor to the children of Israel when that seemed impossible. Favor with man enjoyed by Believers is a gracious gift from our heavenly Father. Apart from Him, we have nothing and we can do nothing (see John 15:5). All we achieve through our own efforts—our own capabilities—may meet our needs and, indeed, make us happy for a season, but it ascribes no glory to God, to whom all glory and honor belongs. Moses was surrounded by a hostile people who had suffered because of the decisions of Pharaoh. But God turned that hostility into favor, and He can do that same thing for you. It is He who lifts you up, who gives you favor with man in the workplace, favor in your business relations—even when it seems that everyone is against you. When it appears that the job market is depressed, God can provide miraculous favor. For whatever task you have been anointed—the door of favor with man will come through favor with God.

—A PRAYER FOR FAVOR—

Father, in the name of Jesus, You make Your face to shine upon me and enlighten me. You are gracious (kind, merciful, and giving favor) to me. I am the head and not the tail, above only and not beneath.

Thank You for Your favor for me because I seek Your Kingdom and Your righteousness and diligently seek good. I am a blessing to You, Lord, and a blessing to _____ (name them: family, neighbors, business associates, etc.). Grace (favor) is with me, because I love the Lord Jesus in sincerity. Because I am Your beloved child, You extend favor, honor, and love to me, so that I am always flowing in Your love, Father. You are pouring out upon me the spirit of favor. You crown me with glory and honor, for I am Your child—Your workmanship.

I am a success today. I am someone very special with You. I am growing in You—waxing strong in spirit. Father, You give me knowledge and skill in all learning and wisdom.

You make me to find favor, compassion, and loving-kindness with _____ (names). I obtain favor in the sight of all who look upon me this day, in the name of Jesus. I am filled with Your fullness—rooted and grounded in love. You are doing exceeding abundantly above all that I ask or think, for Your mighty power is taking over in me.

Thank You, Father, that I am well-favored by You and by man, in Jesus' name! Amen.[16]

—DISCUSSION—
MATERIAL

1. Read Exodus 11.

2. Why did God give the Israelites such favor with the Egyptians?

3. Was this abundance of wealth simply to line the pockets of the Israelites—to pay them back for all the years of hard labor under the harsh reign of Pharaoh?

4. Why do you think God gave Moses favor with Pharaoh despite the fact that Moses had been a fugitive in the land of Egypt?

5. Consider the link between Moses's obedience and his God-given favor.

—SCRIPTURES ON—
BLESSINGS

But my God shall supply all your need according to his riches in glory by Christ Jesus.
PHILIPPIANS 4:19

Every good gift and every perfect gift is from above, and cometh down from the Father of lights, with whom is no variableness, neither shadow of turning.
JAMES 1:17

Give, and it shall be given unto you; good measure, pressed down, and shaken together, and running over, shall men give into your bosom. For with the same measure that ye mete withal it shall be measured to you again.
LUKE 6:38

Beloved, I wish above all things that thou mayest prosper and be in health, even as thy soul prospereth.
3 JOHN 1:2

Fear thou not; for I am with thee: be not dismayed; for I am thy God: I will strengthen thee; yea, I will help thee; yea, I will uphold thee with the right hand of my righteousness.
ISAIAH 41:10

And of his fulness have all we received, and grace for grace.
JOHN 1:16

And said, If thou wilt diligently hearken to the voice of the LORD thy God, and wilt do that which is right in his sight, and wilt give ear to his commandments, and keep all his statutes, I will put none of these diseases upon thee, which I have brought upon the Egyptians: for I am the LORD that healeth thee.
EXODUS 15:26

For it is God which worketh in you both to will and to do of his good pleasure.

PHILIPPIANS 2:13

But if thou shalt indeed obey his voice, and do all that I speak; then I will be an enemy unto thine enemies, and an adversary unto thine adversaries.

EXODUS 23:22

So Jotham became mighty, because he prepared his ways before the LORD his God.

2 CHRONICLES 27:6

And the peace of God, which passeth all understanding, shall keep your hearts and minds through Christ Jesus.

PHILIPPIANS 4:7

Being confident of this very thing, that he which hath begun a good work in you will perform it until the day of Jesus Christ.

PHILIPPIANS 1:6

Now unto him that is able to do exceeding abundantly above all that we ask or think, according to the power that worketh in us.

EPHESIANS 3:20

CHAPTER NINE

PURITY PROMOTES FAVOR

But the LORD was with Joseph and showed him mercy, and He gave him favor in the sight of the keeper of the prison. And the keeper of the prison committed to Joseph's hand all the prisoners who were in the prison; whatever they did there, it was his doing. The keeper of the prison did not look into anything that was under Joseph's authority, because the LORD was with him; and whatever he did, the LORD made it prosper.

—GENESIS 39:21–23

BEST-SELLING AUTHOR and entrepreneur W. Clement Stone wrote:

> Have the courage to say no. Have the courage to face the truth. Do the right thing because it is right. These are the magic keys to living your life with integrity.[17]

My ministry and travels have allowed me to meet many men of integrity. Shortly after the inauguration of President Ronald Reagan in 1985, I was invited to the White House for dinner with eighty-six religious leaders representing the nation. We were deeply moved by the warmth of the president. I was seated next to Chuck Colson. He had been special counsel to former president Richard Nixon and was making his first visit to the White House since Nixon's departure.

During the evening, I turned to Mr. Colson and said, "I imagine your mind is going a mile a minute thinking about the strategy of this meeting." He smiled and said, "No, quite the contrary. I'm going down to death row tonight to share Christ with prisoners who are scheduled to die, and my thoughts are on eternity." Integrity is not the absence of failure; it is the presence of God in the redeemed life.

Joseph's life had not been without failure, but God was able to teach him lessons about integrity and service that would prove invaluable during his lifelong stay in Egypt. As a young man, he was, perhaps, a bit egotistical and boastful, a bit too eager to share his dreams with his jealous brothers. Even then God had a plan and purpose for Joseph's life—one that would come to fruition only after overwhelming and demoralizing obstacles.

The Bible doesn't tell us how long or what humilities Joseph endured at the hands of the Ishmaelite traders after he was sold by his brothers. It is probable that his dirty face was lined by rivulets of tears that snaked their way from his eyes to his chin. It is also likely that he was subjected to indignity, deprivation, and flogging. He awoke one morning to find that the caravan of traders to which he had been sold had reached its destination—a slave market in Egypt, about to be sold once again to the highest bidder. Even so, God granted to him favor with a man from whom he would have had no hope of either mercy or grace.

It was on that fortuitous day that Potiphar, the captain of the palace guard, was striding through the throngs of merchants in search of someone to take on the role of his personal assistant.

Something about Joseph captured his attention. What was different about this young Hebrew? Was he standing to one side of the newly arrived batch of slaves watching as his traveling companions cursed and fought their captors? Did Joseph exude a quiet confidence not seen in the other human offerings? He was, after all, the offspring of Abraham, Isaac, and Jacob—men blessed by Jehovah—an incomparable heritage. Whatever attracted Potiphar to this young man resulted in Joseph being taken home to serve the captain. Genesis 39:2–4 relates:

> The LORD was with Joseph, and he was a success-ful man; and he was in the house of his master the Egyptian. And his master saw that the LORD was with him and that the LORD made all he did to pros-per in his hand. So Joseph found favor in his sight, and served him.

God quickly endowed Joseph with favor so that he avoided some of the more harsh practices to which slaves were subjected—partic-ularly that of castration. Joseph could have wallowed in "might have beens," but instead, he put his shoulder to the wheel and began a life of servitude that continued to win him favor with God and man. He walked with such integrity Potiphar soon discovered that Joseph could be trusted with everything in his house. Genesis 39:5–6 says:

> So it was, from the time that he had made him overseer of his house and all that he had, that the LORD blessed the Egyptian's house for Joseph's sake; and the blessing of the LORD was on all that he had in the house and in the field. Thus he left all that he had

in Joseph's hand, and he did not know what he had
except for the bread which he ate.

As the young Hebrew served his Egyptian master, Potiphar came
to realize that even though he was not a servant of Yahweh, the Most
High God, he was being blessed because of the presence of the son of
Jacob. Joseph refused to take advantage of his master's trust, which
likely did not win him friends among the other servants. This world
could use more men like Joseph—who took his assignment seriously,
worked hard, and lived a life of integrity—no matter the price. How
would you feel if your supervisor approached you to tell you what a
blessing you, as a Christian, were to the organization?

Then, like the snake in the garden, Potiphar's wife reared her
lustful head and tried repeatedly to seduce Joseph. He refused her
advances and, as a result, life changed drastically for him. It is inter-
esting to note that when his wife approached Potiphar and accused
Joseph of assault, her husband didn't immediately have his slave put
to death. Had he more trust in the integrity of Joseph than he did
the veracity of his spouse? No, when you look at the scripture, you
read, "Then Joseph's master took him and put him into the prison, a
place where the king's prisoners were confined" (v. 20). Perhaps that
was the Egyptian equivalent of today's "white collar prison."

Once incarcerated, his sudden and unmerited fall from his
owner's favor had no effect on Joseph's integrity. He continued to
serve Yahweh and the keeper of the prison with equal reliability
and soon had earned the trust of his overseers. Yes, Joseph had been
falsely accused; yes, he had been sentenced to prison. Joseph was
completely unaware of what the future held for him; and although
he had found favor with the warden, he was still a prisoner.

Shortly after being placed in the dungeon, Joseph had an

encounter with both Pharaoh's chief baker and chief butler. Each man's sleep had been interrupted by a disturbing dream, which Joseph had interpreted for them. His only request was to be remembered by the butler when he was restored to his position in the palace. Three days later, the man was released, but it would be two long years before he thought again of the young Hebrew slave who had revealed the future to him.

Joseph, the son of Jacob's beloved wife, Rachel, the one for whom his father had designed a special coat of many colors, was in a place of suffering. Perhaps if he could have captured his feelings on paper, he would have echoed Gerald Sittser whose wife, daughter, and mother died in a tragic automobile accident. He wrote:

> Loss creates a barren present, as if one were sailing on a vast sea of nothingness. Those who suffer loss live suspended between a past for which they long and a future for which they hope. They want to return to the harbor of the familiar past and recover what was lost.... Or they want to sail on and discover a meaningful future that promises to bring them life again .... Instead, they find themselves living in a barren present that is empty of meaning.[18]

What Joseph and many of us fail to realize is that even in the direst circumstances, God can and will turn our mourning into joy and anoint us with favor. Joseph was about to gain favor, not with just any man, but with the Pharaoh over all of Egypt.

Genesis 41:9–16 reveals how Joseph's life was about to change. The butler who had promised to remember his cellmate finally had an epiphany: He realized he had not fulfilled his promise to Joseph:

Then the chief butler spoke to Pharaoh, saying: "I remember my faults this day. When Pharaoh was angry with his servants, and put me in custody in the house of the captain of the guard, both me and the chief baker, we each had a dream in one night, he and I. Each of us dreamed according to the interpretation of his own dream. Now there was a young Hebrew man with us there, a servant of the captain of the guard. And we told him, and he interpreted our dreams for us; to each man he interpreted according to his own dream. And it came to pass, just as he interpreted for us, so it happened. He restored me to my office, and he hanged him." Then Pharaoh sent and called Joseph, and they brought him quickly out of the dungeon; and he shaved, changed his clothing, and came to Pharaoh. And Pharaoh said to Joseph, "I have had a dream, and there is no one who can interpret it. But I have heard it said of you that you can understand a dream, to interpret it." So Joseph answered Pharaoh, saying, "It is not in me; God will give Pharaoh an answer of peace."

On that fateful day, Joseph was going about his daily tasks—dirty, unshaven, clad in rags, and totally unprepared for a divine encounter with Yahweh. When summoned from the prison, imagine his reaction: Was he about to be executed after all this time? Would he be freed only to be sold to a harsh taskmaster? As he responded to the call, he suddenly found that he was to be washed, shaved, and dressed in new garments. He must have been both stunned and confused. Following his spa-like treatment, he was marched from the prison to the palace, where he came face-to-face with Pharaoh, the ruler over all the land.

Joseph had no way of knowing that just the night before, Pharaoh had had a dream that left him unsettled. His magicians and interpreters had failed to render a satisfactory interpretation, so he called for the man recommended by his butler. Joseph listened closely and then, giving all the credit and glory to Yahweh, revealed what was about to happen in the land: seven years of plenty unlike anything ever seen before, followed by seven years of drought that would decimate the land. He wanted Pharaoh to know that the King of Kings and Lord of Lords held the future of Egypt in His divine hand. Then Joseph advised Pharaoh:

> Now therefore, let Pharaoh select a discerning and wise man, and set him over the land of Egypt. Let Pharaoh do this, and let him appoint officers over the land, to collect one-fifth of the produce of the land of Egypt in the seven plentiful years. And let them gather all the food of those good years that are coming, and store up grain under the authority of Pharaoh, and let them keep food in the cities. Then that food shall be as a reserve for the land for the seven years of famine which shall be in the land of Egypt, that the land may not perish during the famine, (Genesis 41:33–36).

Guess who God had prepared to assume the role described? It would be Joseph, the young man standing before him, and Pharaoh made his pronouncement:

"Inasmuch as God has shown you all this, there is no one as discerning and wise as you. You shall be over my house, and all my people shall be ruled according to your word; only in regard to the throne will I be greater than you." And Pharaoh said to Joseph, "See, I have set you over all the land of Egypt." Then Pharaoh took his signet ring off his hand and put it on Joseph's hand; and he clothed him in garments of fine linen and put a gold chain around his neck (vv. 39–42).

Now, that's favor! Joseph had gone from having manacles around his wrists to Pharaoh's ring on his finger—a symbol of power, purpose, and prestige. Noted Christian writer Vance Havner wrote:

> God uses broken things. It takes broken soil to produce a crop, broken clouds to give rain, broken grain to give bread, broken bread to give strength. It is the broken alabaster box that gives forth perfume. It is Peter, weeping bitterly, who returns to greater power than ever.[19]

And, I might add, it took a broken and downcast Joseph to deliver his brethren—and an entire nation—from catastrophe. Joseph had no idea when he awoke that morning in a dank, dirty, and dark dungeon that before day's end, he would be the second most important man in the realm—all because God had given him favor with man. His weeping had endured for a night, but the dawn brought joy and jubilation, peace and promotion. As real as favor with God and man was for Joseph in the land of Egypt, so that same promise is available for the Believer today.

—DISCUSSION—
MATERIAL

1. Read Genesis 39.

2. How had Joseph changed after being sold into slavery?

3. Why did God give him such great favor with Potiphar? The prison warden? Pharoah?

4. Joseph kept himself pure from an entanglement with Potiphar's wife. Why was that important?

5. It seemed that Joseph's decision to remain pure had cost him everything. Consider the ways God blessed him in prison and in the palace.

—SCRIPTURES ON—
PURITY

Let no man despise thy youth; but be thou an example of the believers, in word, in conversation, in charity, in spirit, in faith, in purity.
1 TIMOTHY 4:12

Mortify therefore your members which are upon the earth; fornication, uncleanness, inordinate affection, evil concupiscence, and covetousness, which is idolatry.
COLOSSIANS 3:5

Teaching us that, denying ungodliness and worldly lusts, we should live soberly, righteously, and godly, in this present world.
TITUS 2:12

Wherewithal shall a young man cleanse his way? by taking heed thereto according to thy word.
PSALM 119:9

If we confess our sins, he is faithful and just to forgive us our sins, and to cleanse us from all unrighteousness.
1 JOHN 1:9

Finally, brethren, whatsoever things are true, whatsoever things are honest, whatsoever things are just, whatsoever things are pure, whatsoever things are lovely, whatsoever things are of good report; if there be any virtue, and if there be any praise, think on these things.
PHILIPPIANS 4:8

Marriage is honourable in all, and the bed undefiled: but whoremongers and adulterers God will judge.
HEBREWS 13:4

For this is the will of God, even your sanctification, that ye should abstain from fornication.

1 THESSALONIANS 4:3

Thy word have I hid in mine heart, that I might not sin against thee.

PSALM 119:11

And be not conformed to this world: but be ye transformed by the renewing of your mind, that ye may prove what is that good, and acceptable, and perfect, will of God.

ROMANS 12:2

Wherefore seeing we also are compassed about with so great a cloud of witnesses, let us lay aside every weight, and the sin which doth so easily beset us, and let us run with patience the race that is set before us.

HEBREWS 12:1

Meats for the belly, and the belly for meats: but God shall destroy both it and them. Now the body is not for fornication, but for the Lord; and the Lord for the body.

1 CORINTHIANS 6:13

Blessed are the pure in heart: for they shall see God.

MATTHEW 5:8

CHAPTER TEN

SELFLESSNESS, THE SECRET OF FAVOR

Don't be selfish; don't try to impress others.
Be humble, thinking of others as better than yourselves.

—PHILIPPIANS 2:3 NLT

THE HEBREW WORD *shalom* has several meanings: peace, prosperity, completeness, and it also can be used as hello or good-bye. We tend to think of prosperity in terms of wealth, but it is so much more than that; it is simply "living according to God's principles and experiencing His blessing, and thus, successfully journeying through our pilgrimage here on earth free from greed, worry, and bondage."[20] It affects not only our bank account but also our relationships with others.

True prosperity comes from rich association with others. Poet John Donne wrote, "No man is an island, Entire of itself . . . " A Believer cannot set himself apart from others and fulfill the commandment of Christ to go and tell, to make disciples, and to help those in need. Favor with man comes at a price: No, not in terms of dollars and cents, but in the commitment to learn how to conduct oneself with love and grace and mercy.

If you've read many of my books, you know that my relationship with my siblings has not been free of conflict. As our father lay on his deathbed, I was told by them not to call when he was dying, but to call when he was dead. His abuse had caused years of animosity between him and his children. I alone had cared for him during his declining years, which resulted in my being named sole beneficiary of his will. When meeting with the lawyer after his death and burial, I informed him that I did not wish to inherit and gave instructions to divide any remaining assets between my siblings. I then wrote informing them of my decision. It was an attempt to reconnect with my brothers and sisters. It would have been well within my purview to pocket whatever was left, but that was not what God required of me.

It was after returning home from the funeral that God began to give me unprecedented favor with a group of men whom I would never have been able to reach otherwise. During a trip to New York City immediately afterward, I was able to meet with then president of Iran, Mahmoud Ahmadinejad, and arrange a Fox News Network interview with him. Favor and blessings followed obedience.

According to Acts 2:47, early Believers were "praising God and having favor with all the people." The men and women who were followers of Christ lived lives glorifying God and blessing others. Their lives exuded worship and exaltation of our Lord and Savior.

Let's look at some of the practices we can adopt that will produce favor with man. First, we can show a genuine interest in others. This is not a "Hi, how are you?" approach. It means giving personal attention to people. In Philippians 2:4 (NLT), the apostle Paul gave us this guideline: "Don't look out only for your own interests, but take an interest in others, too."

This is not a self-centered, me-first attitude, but a real attentiveness to others—what they have to say. It is listening intently and responding appropriately. An example would be Jesus and the woman at the well. He could have ignored her, but instead He chose to connect with her. It was an unprecedented step for a Jew to engage in conversation with a Samaritan. It was a social taboo for a man to be seen talking openly with an unknown female. It could have been misconstrued as an open invitation to a woman with loose morals, which would have reflected badly on Jesus.

But there was even more fodder for the gossips: This woman was a known adulteress in the community. Her trip to the well in the middle of the afternoon was an attempt to avoid interacting with other women in the village. We are not certain that she was a prostitute, but that would have mattered little given what we do know: She had been married five times and was at that moment living with someone outside marriage. The woman was an outcast who found little favor with God or man.

Mark Hall of the Christian band Casting Crowns penned the lyrics to a song that could have been written about this woman. It is titled, "Does Anybody Care." Hall wrote:

> Does anybody hear her? Can anybody see?
> If judgment looms under every steeple
> If lofty glances from lofty people
> Can't see past her scarlet letter
> And we've never even met her
> Never even met her, never even met her
> Does anybody hear her? Does anybody see?[21]

Jesus saw her as she approached the well and was overcome with such great compassion that He spoke to her. Has that ever happened to you? Have you ever felt compelled by the Holy Spirit to approach someone? Jesus struck up a conversation and then offered her eternal life—living water. If she accepted, He told her, she would never thirst again. She was offered a never-ending source of supply—from Him who is the Living Water—and Jesus gave her favor with all those in the village who had rejected her:

> The woman then left her waterpot, went her way into the city, and said to the men, "Come, see a Man who told me all things that I ever did. Could this be the Christ?" Then they went out of the city and came to Him (John 4:28–30).

When she shared the message of the Good News, they were not only willing to associate with her but followed her back to the source of her joy—the Man waiting at the well. This woman had found it impossible to spend time with Jesus and not be changed. She might have shunned Him; she could have turned away as bereft as she was when she first arrived at the well, but she did not. The woman chose to accept the message of love and grace that Jesus offered and her life was changed.

Secondly, a cheerful countenance will win favor with man. Nobody wants to talk to a grouch! God can provide favor with man, but you have to put that smile on your face. Proverbs 17:22 (NIV) says, "A cheerful heart is good medicine, but a crushed spirit dries up the bones."

We must not downplay the value of a smile:

It costs nothing, but creates much good. It enriches those who receive it without impoverishing those who give it away. It happens in a flash but the memory of it can last forever. No one is so rich that he can get along without it. No one is too poor to feel rich when receiving it. It creates happiness in the home, fosters good will in business, and is the countersign of friends. It is rest to the weary, daylight to the discouraged, sunshine to the sad, and nature's best antidote for trouble.[22]

The world is drawn to those who wear an authentic smile. In the 1920s Otis Deaton and M. L. Yandell wrote a song titled, "Give the World a Smile." The lilting chorus reads:

> Give the world a smile each day
> Helping someone on life's way
> From the paths of sin oh bring the wanderers in
> To the master's fold to stay
> Help to cheer the lone and sad
> Help to make some pilgrim glad
> Let your life so be that all the world might see
> The joy of serving Jesus with a smile.[23]

A pastor of my acquaintance once quipped that he would begin jogging when he saw more joggers smiling. Could that same edict hold true of the world? Will more people be drawn to Jesus and the message of the gospel when they see Believers smiling with true joy? You and I have every reason to smile, even when pain, pressure, and problems are mounting. We have the assurance of God's grace in this life and eternity with Jesus in the life to come. Favor with man can be boosted by a smile. Try it; it works. Mother Teresa once advised, "Every time you smile at someone, it is an action of love, a gift to that person, a beautiful thing."[24]

Thirdly, you can win favor with man by being slow to speak your mind. How often do people tune us out because we are quick to harshly offer our opinions? Michael Nichols, a therapist wrote a book titled *The Lost Art of Listening*. In it he states:

> Listening is so basic that we take it for granted. Unfortunately, most of us think of ourselves as better listeners than we really are.[25]

In his book *Growing Strong in the Seasons of Life*, pastor, teacher, and author Charles Swindoll wrote a chapter titled "Dialogues of the Deaf." In it he quoted Swiss psychiatrist Paul Tournier:

> It is impossible to overemphasize the immense need humans have to be really listened to, to be taken seriously, to be understood. No one can develop freely in this world and find a full life without feeling understood by at least one other person . . . [26]

Swindoll goes on to ask:

> Have you ever practiced listening evangelism? . . . Sure the gospel must ultimately be shared, but taking time to listen patiently and respond calmly is an essential part of the process.[27]

We often hear the phrase "Listen carefully." To gain favor with man, we must develop the gift of careful listening—not only with our ears but with our eyes and with our hearts. Really hearing what another person has to say is not sitting on the edge of your seat eagerly planning your rebuttal, or interrupting to inject your own comment. It is waiting, sometimes while silence fills the room, giving your friend, spouse, or acquaintance time to marshal their thoughts and find the words to express their hurt, fear, anger, or hopelessness. That was what Jesus did so lovingly during His encounter with the woman at the well. He knew her past, present, and future, yet He gave her space to bare her soul to the only One who could change her life.

You and I have the answer to the question, "Lord, to whom shall we go?" (See John 6:68.) You and I have been entrusted with the Good News—the gospel of Jesus Christ. In order to help others find that answer, we must cultivate the art of listening. Luke 8:18 (NIV) reads, "Therefore consider carefully how you listen." And Matthew 11:15 (NLT) admonishes, "Anyone with ears to hear should listen and understand!" Cultivate listening and as you do, God will bless you with favor among those who desperately need to hear about the gift of salvation and the One who brought it to us.

According to James 1:19, listening also has another dimension, "So then, my beloved brethren, let every man be swift to hear, slow to speak, slow to wrath."

In my book about relationships, *Turning Your Pain Into Gain*, I wrote about how words affect us:

> Pay close attention to what you allow to enter and
> fill your heart, for "out of the fullness (the overflow,

the superabundance) of the heart the mouth speaks"
(Matthew 12:34 AMP).

If you allow your heart to be filled with contaminating thoughts
and feelings of bitterness, blame, self-pity, condemnation and fear,
don't be surprised when your mouth overflows with words of rejection, hatred, mistrust and insecurity.

Closely monitor and guard what you think in your heart. The
Scriptures reveal a vital, but often ignored, principle concerning the
importance of our thoughts. Proverbs 23:7 declares that "As a man
thinks in his heart, so is he."

Thoughts shape the soul. We can use words and actions to con-
ceal, counterfeit, and misrepresent, but all the time our thoughts are
determining who we are and what we will become. We are either
being built up or destroyed from within.

For years my mind replayed my father's rejection and ridicule
until I accepted it and repeated it to myself. Then I discovered that
if I wanted to silence the nagging, negative voice within and replace
it with a strengthening, encouraging winner's voice, my heart had
to be filled with and focused on the healing and life-giving words of
my heavenly Father.

All too often disagreements can be averted if we simply heed
the words of James 1:19. It was Solomon who admonished, "A soft
answer turns away wrath, but a harsh word stirs up anger." God can
bless us with favor with man, but you and I must do our part—first
by listening and then by speaking words sprinkled with kindness.

Next, when you do speak, encourage. What precisely does that
mean? The Merriam-Webster definition is, "to inspire with courage,
spirit, or hope, hearten." We are human beings; God created us

with the need for encouragement. Do you know someone who is pessimistic; who always seems to have a dark cloud hovering over them—who sees the glass as half empty, all the time? An unknown author said, "A pessimist's blood type is always B-negative."[28]

On the night before His crucifixion, Jesus invited the disciples to go with Him to the garden of Gethsemane to watch and pray. Totally God and totally man, Jesus needed the closeness and encouragement of His friends as He prepared to face His darkest hour. We, too, are surrounded by people who need encouragement in their darkest hour, and the blessing of favor with man allows us the opportunity to "Bear one another's burdens, and so fulfill the law of Christ" (Galatians 6:2).

It is important that we are ready and willing to offer encouragement when needed. When the world is screaming, "Oh, God, we're all going to die," the Believer should be ready to share the hope that is within him. To do that, we must be sincerely concerned about others rather than plot how those relationships can best benefit us. There is power in encouragement; it has the capacity to change lives when coupled with the message of hope and salvation. In his letter to the Romans, Paul admonishes us:

> Be kindly affectionate to one another with brotherly love, in honor giving preference to one another; not lagging in diligence, fervent in spirit, serving the Lord; rejoicing in hope, patient in tribulation, continuing steadfastly in prayer; distributing to the needs of the saints, given to hospitality . . . . Rejoice with those who rejoice, and weep with those who weep (Romans 12:10–13, 15).

With favor comes responsibility; ask the Lord today what you can do to encourage someone—make a phone call, send an email, write a letter, invite a friend to lunch or for coffee. Oh, and don't forget to say, "I love you," to the people who mean the most to you, and treat all men with courtesy and appreciation. Encouragement and optimism will go a long way when God gives you favor with man.

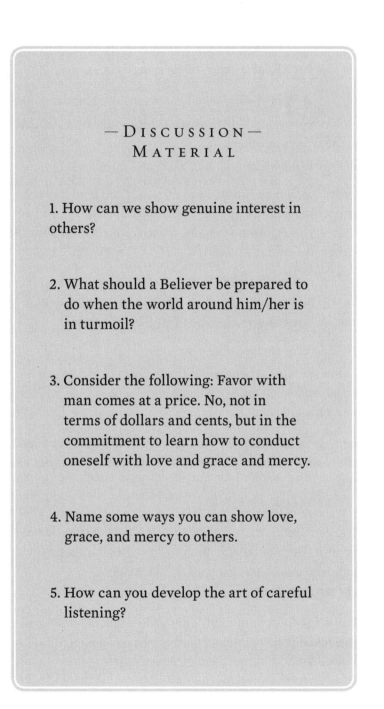

— DISCUSSION —
MATERIAL

1. How can we show genuine interest in others?

2. What should a Believer be prepared to do when the world around him/her is in turmoil?

3. Consider the following: Favor with man comes at a price. No, not in terms of dollars and cents, but in the commitment to learn how to conduct oneself with love and grace and mercy.

4. Name some ways you can show love, grace, and mercy to others.

5. How can you develop the art of careful listening?

— S C R I P T U R E S   O N —
S E L F L E S S N E S S

Look not every man on his own things, but every man also on the things of others.
PHILIPPIANS 2:4

But love ye your enemies, and do good, and lend, hoping for nothing again; and your reward shall be great, and ye shall be the children of the Highest: for he is kind unto the unthankful and to the evil.
LUKE 6:35

Finally, be ye all of one mind, having compassion one of another, love as brethren, be pitiful, be courteous.
1 PETER 3:8

And beside this, giving all diligence, add to your faith virtue; and to virtue knowledge.
2 PETER 1:5

See that none render evil for evil unto any man; but ever follow that which is good, both among yourselves, and to all men.
1 THESSALONIANS 5:15

Charge them that are rich in this world, that they be not highminded, nor trust in uncertain riches, but in the living God, who giveth us richly all things to enjoy.
1 TIMOTHY 6:17

This is my commandment, That ye love one another, as I have loved you.
JOHN 15:12

Let your conversation be without covetousness; and be content with such things as ye have: for he hath said, I will never leave thee, nor forsake thee.

HEBREWS 13:5

For God so loved the world, that he gave his only begotten Son, that whosoever believeth in him should not perish, but have everlasting life.

JOHN 3:16

For it is God which worketh in you both to will and to do of his good pleasure.

PHILIPPIANS 2:13

Finally, brethren, whatsoever things are true, whatsoever things are honest, whatsoever things are just, whatsoever things are pure, whatsoever things are lovely, whatsoever things are of good report; if there be any virtue, and if there be any praise, think on these things.

PHILIPPIANS 4:8

Herein is love, not that we loved God, but that he loved us, and sent his Son to be the propitiation for our sins.

1 JOHN 4:10

For all the law is fulfilled in one word, even in this; Thou shalt love thy neighbour as thyself.

GALATIANS 5:14

CHAPTER ELEVEN

⁂

FAVOR OF MAN
FOR THE
TASK AT HAND

Now Hiram king of Tyre sent his servants to Solomon,
because he heard that they had anointed him king in place
of his father, for Hiram had always loved David.

—1 KINGS 5:1

WHEN KING SOLOMON wrote in Proverbs 22:1, "A *good* name is to be chosen rather than great riches, loving favor rather than silver and gold," perhaps he was thinking of his father, David. A good name and favor would be of paramount importance as David planned his life's work and heart's desire: building a temple to house the ark of the covenant. The shepherd who had slain Goliath and then had run for his life from King Saul had finally consolidated Judah and Israel into one united kingdom.

The ark had been captured by the Philistines when Samuel was a child, and even the defeat of Goliath and the rout of the enemy did not secure a return of the symbol of God's presence. The ark had been paraded throughout the Philistine territory with trouble and disease following the desecration of the holy emblem. Finally, with the lesson learned, the ark was returned to the Israelites and housed at Kirjath Jearim, a village west of Jerusalem. First Samuel 7:1 tells us, "Then the men of Kirjath Jearim came and took the ark of the LORD, and brought it into the house of Abinadab on the hill, and consecrated Eleazar his son to keep the ark of the LORD." It resided there until after the deaths of Samuel and King Saul. After an initial aborted attempt to move the ark to Jerusalem (see 2 Samuel 6), it was left in the home of Obed-Edom. We then read in 2 Samuel 6:12–15:

> Now it was told King David, saying, "The LORD has blessed the house of Obed-Edom and all that belongs to him, because of the ark of God." So David went and brought up the ark of God from the house of Obed-Edom to the City of David with gladness. And so it was, when those bearing the ark of the LORD had gone six paces, that he sacrificed oxen and fatted sheep. Then David danced before the LORD with all his might; and David was wearing a linen ephod. So David and all the house of Israel brought up the ark of the LORD with shouting and with the sound of the trumpet.

The ark of the covenant had been returned to the City of David, and now rested in the Tent of Meeting that was the heart of worship in Israel. This had been God's symbolic dwelling place during the trek though the wilderness. David realized that while he lived in a palace constructed of the finest cedars from Lebanon and built by the most talented craftsmen provided by his friend King Hiram of Tyre—a Phoenician city north of Carmel—Jehovah's dwelling place was a tent! How ludicrous that must have seemed to a man who had risen through the ranks from sheep pen to palace.

With that realization, David began to make plans to build a temple for Jehovah. When he shared his building proposal with Nathan, the prophet, Nathan gave him a hearty thumbs-up—at least before he went home and retired for the night. As he slept, the Spirit of God spoke to him and said:

> "Go and tell my servant David, 'This is what the LORD says: Are you the one to build me a house to dwell in? I have not dwelt in a house from the day I brought the Israelites up out of Egypt to this day. I have been moving from place to place with a tent as my dwelling. Wherever I have moved with all the Israelites, did I ever say to any of their rulers whom I commanded to shepherd my people Israel, "Why have you not built me a house of cedar?"' "Now then, tell my servant David, 'This is what the LORD Almighty says: I took you from the pasture, from tending the flock, and appointed you ruler over my people Israel. I have been with you wherever you have gone, and I have cut off all your enemies from before you. Now I will make your name great, like the names of the greatest men on earth. And I will provide a place for my people Israel and will plant them so that they can have a home of their own and no longer be disturbed. Wicked people will not oppress them anymore, as they did at the beginning and have done ever since the time I appointed leaders over my people Israel. I will also give you rest from all your enemies. "'The LORD

declares to you that the LORD himself will establish a house for you: When your days are over and you rest with your ancestors, I will raise up your offspring to succeed you, your own flesh and blood, and I will establish his kingdom. He is the one who will build a house for my Name, and I will establish the throne of his kingdom forever. I will be his father, and he will be my son. When he does wrong, I will punish him with a rod wielded by men, with floggings inflicted by human hands. But my love will never be taken away from him, as I took it away from Saul, whom I removed from before you. Your house and your kingdom will endure forever before me; your throne will be established forever.'" (2 Samuel 7:5–16).

God wanted David to know that He really didn't need a house made of cedar and stone. He wanted His home to be within the hearts of His people Israel. Never had Jehovah asked for a place of residence; He had asked for commitment, honesty, kindness, loyalty, mercy. He required His people to honor their parents, to remember the Sabbath day and keep it holy. He commanded that they not commit adultery, murder, covet, lie, or steal; but never had He demanded, "I want a palatial palace."

Author and Pastor Eugene Peterson wrote:

> But there are times when our grand human plans to do something for God are seen, after a night of prayer, to be a huge human distraction from what God is doing for us. That's what Nathan realized that night: God showed Nathan that David's building plans

for God would interfere with God's building plans for David.[29]

Peterson then boils it down to the nitty-gritty:

> The message that Nathan delivers to David is dominated by a recital of what God has done, is doing, and will do. God is the first-person subject of twenty-three verbs in this message, and these verbs carry the action. David, full of what he's going to do for God, is now subjected to a comprehensive rehearsal of what God has done, is doing, and will do for and in David. What looked yesterday like a bold Davidic enterprise on behalf of God now looks picayune.[30]

David's leadership acumen and favor with those surrounding him enabled him to build a united country with Jerusalem as its center of religious influence. It became a shining inspiration as a city, but God was more interested in the holiness of its inhabitants. The easy part was the building; the more difficult proposition was its people. All these centuries later, the first and second temples are in ruins, the beautiful implements lost to the Jews. There is, however, a remnant—spiritual descendants—of the house of David to this day.

While David was king and even after God had forbidden him to begin work on the temple, he began to gather and stockpile the materials that would be needed by Solomon to build the house of God in Jerusalem. It would be years later before God revealed to David the reason He withheld the task of building the temple from the "man after God's own heart," (see 1 Samuel 13).

In 1 Chronicles 28:3, God admonished David:

You shall not build a house for My name, because you have been a man of war and have shed blood.

After the death of his father, David, King Solomon issued the mandate for construction and work began on the temple site. Actually, it was King Hiram of Tyre who first reached out to Solomon. In 1 Kings 5:1–7:

> Now Hiram king of Tyre sent his servants to Solomon, because he heard that they had anointed him king in place of his father, for Hiram had always loved David. Then Solomon sent to Hiram, saying: You know how my father David could not build a house for the name of the LORD his God because of the wars which were fought against him on every side, until the LORD put his foes under the soles of his feet. But now the LORD my God has given me rest on every side; there is neither adversary nor evil occurrence. And behold, I propose to build a house for the name of the LORD my God, as the LORD spoke to my father David, saying, "Your son, whom I will set on your throne in your place, he shall build the house for My name." Now therefore, command that they cut down cedars for me from Lebanon; and my servants will be with your servants, and I will pay you wages for your servants according to whatever you say. For you know there is none among us who has skill to cut timber like the Sidonians. So it was, when Hiram heard the words of Solomon, that he rejoiced greatly and said,

Blessed be the LORD this day, for He has given David
a wise son over this great people!

Solomon responded to Hiram by telling him that he desired to
build a house for the Lord. Hiram responded by honoring David for
raising such a wise son, and the two covenanted together to build.
Solomon realized that Hiram owned the most skilled laborers in the
region, and the two would work together to see David's dream come
to fruition. Solomon sent his "shopping list" to Hiram.

Solomon found favor in Hiram's sight, and the two men worked
together to bless the Lord of Hosts by erecting a dwelling place for
Jehovah-Tsidkenu—the Lord my Righteousness!

—DISCUSSION—
MATERIAL

1. Read 2 Samuel 6–7.

2. Why was David forbidden to build the Temple? How did he respond?

3. David cultivated friends and associates. How long has it been since you reached out to someone on the fringes of your circle of friends?

4. Jehovah had never asked for a grand home. What had He asked for instead?

5. Consider the following: David was nation building; God was building His people. What does this mean to you?

—scriptures on—
Being Equipped
for Service

I have shewed you all things, how that so labouring ye ought to support the weak, and to remember the words of the Lord Jesus, how he said, It is more blessed to give than to receive.

Acts 20:35

And whatsoever ye do in word or deed, do all in the name of the Lord Jesus, giving thanks to God and the Father by him.

Colossians 3:17

Yea, a man may say, Thou hast faith, and I have works: shew me thy faith without thy works, and I will shew thee my faith by my works.

James 2:18

For, brethren, ye have been called unto liberty; only use not liberty for an occasion to the flesh, but by love serve one another.

Galatians 5:13

For as the body without the spirit is dead, so faith without works is dead also.

James 2:26

Take heed that ye do not your alms before men, to be seen of them: otherwise ye have no reward of your Father which is in heaven.

Matthew 6:1

The liberal soul shall be made fat: and he that watereth shall be watered also himself.

Proverbs 11:25

Let him that stole steal no more: but rather let him labour, working with his hands the thing which is good, that he may have to give to him that needeth.

EPHESIANS 4:28

For I was an hungred, and ye gave me meat: I was thirsty, and ye gave me drink: I was a stranger, and ye took me in.

MATTHEW 25:35

Therefore to him that knoweth to do good, and doeth it not, to him it is sin.

JAMES 4:17

Servants, be obedient to them that are your masters according to the flesh, with fear and trembling, in singleness of your heart, as unto Christ.

EPHESIANS 6:5

For we are his workmanship, created in Christ Jesus unto good works, which God hath before ordained that we should walk in them.

EPHESIANS 2:10

And he sat down, and called the twelve, and saith unto them, If any man desire to be first, the same shall be last of all, and servant of all.

MARK 9:35

CHILDREN, OBEY YOUR PARENTS IN THE LORD: FOR THIS IS RIGHT.

EPHESIANS 6:1

Though I speak with the tongues of men and of angels, and have not charity, I am become as sounding brass, or a tinkling cymbal.

1 CORINTHIANS 13:1

PART TWO

THE
CHARACTERISTICS
OF FAVOR

*But the fruit of the Spirit is love, joy,
peace, longsuffering, gentleness, goodness,
faith, meekness, temperance . . .*

(GALATIANS 5:22–23 KJV)

CHAPTER TWELVE

LOVE

But the fruit of the Spirit is love . . .

—GALATIANS 5:22

IN 1965 POPULAR COMPOSER Burt Bacharach and lyricist Hal David wrote a hit song: "What the World Needs Now Is Love." The opening lines of that catchy tune are:

> What the world needs now is love, sweet love
> It's the only thing that there's just too little of
> What the world needs now is love, sweet love
> No not just for some but for everyone.[31]

As Believers, God has called us to demonstrate His love to others with overt acts of love. It is often the smallest, simplest, and most ordinary deeds that have the greatest impact on a world starved for kindness.

One day, as I was praying in my hotel room in Boston, in the Spirit I saw a man on his knees with his head resting on a basketball. He was weeping and obviously distraught. The Holy Spirit whispered to me, *"Go downstairs to the restaurant. You are to witness to that man."* I had no idea who the individual was, but I followed the Lord's leading. I went to the restaurant, and a basketball player who had been with the Boston Celtics caught me by surprise when he walked up to me and said, "Man, I love you! When you shared the gospel at a pregame chapel, I was saved. Then God saved my marriage, my career, and my life. I've always wanted to thank you. God Bless you."

I smiled and thanked God for sending me downstairs, thinking that was that. Then the restaurant filled with some of the most famous basketball players in the United States. When the waiter brought my check, Jesus softly instructed, *"Pay their bill."*

I thought, *Lord, they're millionaire basketball players!*

Again, that still small voice said, *"Pay their bill."* There must have been over twenty players in that room and I had watched them eat huge breakfasts!

"Pay their bill." So I swallowed the lump in my throat and asked for their check.

That afternoon, one of the players sent someone over to thank me, inviting me to dinner to return the favor. Over dinner, I shared the gospel with Michael Jordan and was able to tell him of God's love extended to us through His Son, Jesus Christ.

What the world needs is not the fake, promiscuous, Hollywood-tinged lust that is passed off as love, but rather *agape* love. According to one definition (paraphrased):

> Agape means to choose to seek the best for others. This is a love based in the mind. We can *choose* to show agape love by actively thinking about, and deciding how we act toward other people. Agape is

the word used when the Bible talks about Christian love for one another. Agape love is talking about our behavior towards others, not our feelings. Phileo love is about feelings. Agape love is about how we act toward others.[32]

Favor with man will come when we choose to show God's love to others with *their* good in mind, not ours. It can be as unassuming as a smile, a cup of water, buying a burger for a stranger, or offering to help a harried mother with her bags. Agape takes many forms and can change lives in the process. Just as Jesus spoke to His disciples in Matthew 10 and Mark 9 about giving a cup of water, it's not just about providing liquid refreshment; no, it is about giving ourselves—inconveniencing *me* to help someone else.

Relationship with God and man is built by one act of kindness laid on another. One such simple act of agape led to my meeting my most beloved heroine, Corrie ten Boom. She was carrying her bags into a hotel in Northeast Texas when I approached, asking her if I could be of assistance. She said no, but then invited me to share a meager meal with her. It was the beginning of a lifelong relationship.

The story is told of a lowly desk clerk in a backstreet hotel in Philadelphia:

> Into it one night there came two tired elderly people. They went up to the night clerk and the husband pleadingly said, "Mister, please don't tell us you don't have a room. My wife and I have been all over the city looking for a place to stay. We didn't know about the big conventions that are here. The hotels at which we usually stay are all full. We're dead tired

and it's after midnight. Please, don't tell us you don't have a place where we can sleep."

The clerk looked at them a long moment and then answered, "Well, I don't have a single room except my own. I work at night and sleep in the daytime. It's not as nice as the other rooms, but it's clean, and I'll be happy for you to be my guests for tonight."

The wife said, "God bless you, young man."

The next morning at the breakfast table, the couple sent the waiter to tell the night clerk they wanted to see him on very important business. The night clerk went in, recognized the two people, sat down at the table and said he hoped they had had a good night's sleep. They thanked him most sincerely. Then the husband astounded the clerk with this statement: "You're too fine a hotel man to stay in a hotel like this. How would you like for me to build a big, beautiful, luxurious hotel in the city of New York and make you general manager?"

The clerk didn't know what to say. He thought there might be something wrong with their minds. He finally stammered, "It sounds wonderful." His guest then introduced himself. "I'm John Jacob Astor." So, the Waldorf-Astoria Hotel was built.[33]

True to his promise, Mr. Astor rewarded the generosity of the night clerk, who became manager of the hotel. His kindness brought him favor with one of the richest men in the United States. Deeds should not be done with expectations of grand returns, but the most modest of endeavors can touch the hearts of strangers and produce eternal rewards.

Opportunities to show agape love to others may not come our way each day, but when they do we need to react with love and grace. And acts of kindness can be contagious. The expression "Pay it forward" was first introduced into the American fabric in 1916 in the Lily Hardy Hammond book *In the Garden of Delight*.[34]

Catherine Ryan Hyde titled her novel released in 2000, *Pay It Forward*. According to background information on the book, it is:

An obligation to do three good deeds for others in response to a good deed that one receives. Such good deeds should accomplish things that the other person cannot accomplish on their own. In this way, the practice of helping one another can spread geometrically through society, at a ratio of three to one, creating a social movement with an impact of making the world a better place. The Pay it Forward Movement and Foundation was founded in the USA helping start a ripple effect of kindness acts around the world.[35]

In reality, what Ms. Hammond and Ms. Hyde saw as a catch-phrase and a movement was introduced by a lowly carpenter some 2,000 years ago when Jesus said, "Do to others as you want them to do to you." We sometimes call it the "Golden Rule."

A wonderful Christmas story took place at Lakewood Elementary School in Dallas in 2014. Nathaniel Kendrick, a school crossing guard had lovingly watched over the neighborhood kids twice daily as they went to and from class. A reporter detailed what happened on this special day:

> According to local news outlet WFAA-TV, Kendrick, whose wife is ill, has been struggling financially. Recently, his car was repossessed. Little did he know, however, that he'd soon be in for a huge surprise. While Kendrick was working one day, a group of dads from Friends of Lakewood, a local parent group, parked a new car in the middle of the street. The crossing guard asked them to move the car, but the dads refused. "It's your car," they said, handing him the keys. "So [you] get it out of the crosswalk."
>
> Kendrick stared at them for a long time, totally flabbergasted and overwhelmed with emotion, as the news sunk in. After hearing about Kendrick's plight, the Friends of Lakewood dads had decided to start fundraising to buy the crossing guard a new car. They are said to have raised enough in just a week.[36]

What a wonderful way to "pay it forward"!

Exceptional circumstances are not obvious to us every day, but a smile is free. Patience with a harried server or clerk costs us nothing. "A kind word fitly spoken," said King Solomon in Proverbs 25:11, "is like apples of gold in settings of silver."

As Jesus was teaching in the temple one day, a lawyer approached him with the question, "What is the greatest commandment of all?"

Jesus replied:

"'You shall love the LORD your God with all your heart, with all your soul, and with all your mind.' This is the first and great commandment. And the second is like it: 'You shall love your neighbor as yourself.' On these two commandments hang all the Law and the Prophets," (Matthew 22:37–40).

In Romans 13:8–10, the apostle Paul wrote:

Owe no one anything except to love one another, for he who loves another has fulfilled the law. For the commandments, "You shall not commit adultery," "You shall not murder," "You shall not steal," "You shall not bear false witness," "You shall not covet," and if there is any other commandment, are all summed up in this saying, namely, "You shall love your neighbor as yourself." Love does no harm to a neighbor; therefore love is the fulfillment of the law.

In Luke 6:30–36, Jesus expounds on His commandment to "do unto others" by saying:

Give to everyone who asks of you. And from him who takes away your goods do not ask them back. And just as you want men to do to you, you also do to them likewise. But if you love those who love you, what credit is that to you? For even sinners love those who love them. And if you do good to those who do good to you, what credit is that to you? For even sinners do the same. And if you lend to those from whom you hope to receive back, what credit is that to you? For even sinners lend to sinners to receive as much back. But love your enemies, do good, and lend, hoping for nothing in return; and your reward will be great, and you will be sons of the Most High. For He is kind to the unthankful and evil. Therefore be merciful, just as your Father also is merciful.

How long has it been since you've invited a struggling officemate for lunch or a round of golf? Or called a grieving friend to meet for coffee? Or slipped an envelope to someone you know who is struggling financially? Listen to the voice of the Holy Spirit and be ready to reach out as He directs. Consider: What would you want someone to do for you if you were in their situation? Or what has someone done for you in similar circumstances? Respond with agape love, mercy, and charity.

The great Swiss theologian and philosopher, Dr. Karl Barth, was invited to lecture in the United States. Dr. Billy Graham tells the story:

> While he was in this country, a student at one of the seminaries said, "Dr. Barth, what is the greatest truth that ever crossed your mind?" All the seminary students were sitting on the edge of their seats to hear some great, profound, deep, complicated answer. Dr. Barth slowly raised his great shaggy gray head and looked at the student and said, "Jesus loves me, this I know, for the Bible tells me so."[37]

The greatest act of kindness you and I could ever do is to tell someone the story of God's love from John 3:16:

> For God so loved the world that He gave His only
> begotten Son, that whoever believes in Him should
> not perish but have everlasting life.

Two of the greatest needs of mankind are forgiveness and love. God offered both through His Son, Jesus Christ. It has been said that a human being has a God-shaped hole in his heart, a place that can only be filled with a relationship with his Creator. It is a spiritual law written on a tablet of flesh. When we reach out in love with the message of the gospel, those with whom we come in contact can be pointed to the answer of how to fill that void. Can you hear Paul shout in 2 Corinthians 9:15: "Thanks be to God for His indescribable gift!"

You and I are not asked to "leap tall buildings in a single bound," or perform mighty miracles; we are simply called upon to reflect the love of God in our daily words and deeds. What is most important is the motivation with which we serve. First John 4:10–11 tells us:

> In this is love, not that we have loved God, but that
> He loved us and sent His Son to be the propitiation for
> our sins. Beloved, if God so loved us, we also ought to
> love one another.

To love as Christ loves will bring favor with man—for that kind of love is not an emotion; it is a living reality.

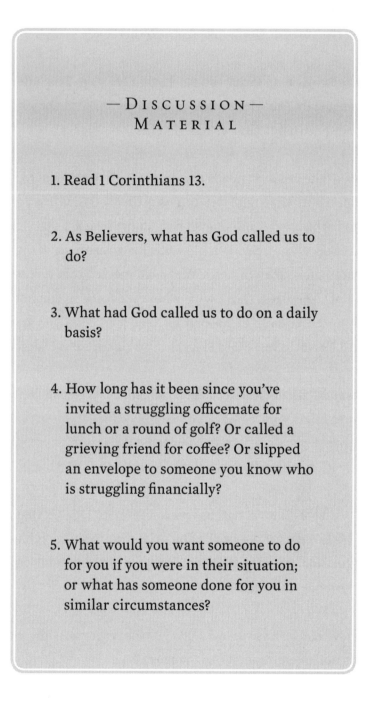

—DISCUSSION—
MATERIAL

1. Read 1 Corinthians 13.

2. As Believers, what has God called us to do?

3. What had God called us to do on a daily basis?

4. How long has it been since you've invited a struggling officemate for lunch or a round of golf? Or called a grieving friend for coffee? Or slipped an envelope to someone you know who is struggling financially?

5. What would you want someone to do for you if you were in their situation; or what has someone done for you in similar circumstances?

—SCRIPTURES ON—
LOVE

And thou shalt love the LORD thy God with all thine heart, and with all thy soul, and with all thy might.
DEUTERONOMY 6:5

Jesus said unto him, Thou shalt love the Lord thy God with all thy heart, and with all thy soul, and with all thy mind.
MATTHEW 22:37

Let all your things be done with charity.
1 CORINTHIANS 16:14

He that loveth not knoweth not God; for God is love.
1 JOHN 4:8

We love him, because he first loved us.
1 JOHN 4:19

No man hath seen God at any time. If we love one another, God dwelleth in us, and his love is perfected in us.
1 JOHN 4:12

There is no fear in love; but perfect love casteth out fear: because fear hath torment. He that feareth is not made perfect in love.
1 JOHN 4:18

And thou shalt love the Lord thy God with all thy heart, and with all thy soul, and with all thy mind, and with all thy strength: this is the first commandment.
MARK 12:30

And now abideth faith, hope, charity, these three; but the greatest of these is charity.

1 CORINTHIANS 13:13

If ye love me, keep my commandments.
JOHN 14:15

For God so loved the world, that he gave his only begotten Son, that whosoever believeth in him should not perish, but have everlasting life.
JOHN 3:16

And above all things have fervent charity among yourselves: for charity shall cover the multitude of sins.
1 PETER 4:8

Beloved, let us love one another: for love is of God; and every one that loveth is born of God, and knoweth God.
1 JOHN 4:7

And this I pray, that your love may abound yet more and more in knowledge and in all judgment.
PHILIPPIANS 1:9

And be ye kind one to another, tenderhearted, forgiving one another, even as God for Christ's sake hath forgiven you.
EPHESIANS 4:32

JOY

A cheerful disposition is good for your health;
gloom and doom leave you bone-tired.

—PROVERBS 17:22 MSG

RECENTLY, I READ THE STORY of Patrick Henry Hughes. It is an amazing testament of the enormous favor a joy-filled life can bring:

He was rolled onto the stage in his wheelchair, and began to play the piano. His fingers danced across the keys as he made beautiful music.

He then began to sing as he played, and it was even more beautiful . . . . There was this aura about him . . . his smile was magic! About ten minutes into Patrick's performance, someone came on the stage and said . . . "I'd like to share a seven-minute video titled, The Patrick Henry Hughes story." And the lights went dim.

Patrick Henry Hughes was born with no eyes, and a tightening of the joints which left him crippled for life. However, as a child, he was fitted with artificial eyes and placed in a wheelchair. Before his first birthday, he discovered the piano. His mom said, "I could hit any note on the piano, and within one or two tries, he'd get it." By his second birthday, he was playing requests (You Are My Sunshine, Twinkle Twinkle Little Star). His father was ecstatic. "We might not play baseball, but we can play music together."

[At the] University of Louisville . . . He's also a part of the 214-member marching band. You read it right . . . the marching band! He's a blind, wheelchair-bound trumpet player; and he and his father do it together. They attend all the band practices and the half-time performance in front of thousands. His father rolls and rotates his son around the field to the cheers of Patrick's fans. In order to attend Patrick's classes and every band practice, his father works the graveyard shift at UPS. Patrick said . . . "My dad's my hero."

But even more than his unbelievable musical talent, it was Patrick's "attitude of gratitude" that touched my soul. On stage, between songs, he would talk to the audience about his life and about how blessed he was. He said, "God made me blind and unable to walk. BIG DEAL! He gave me the ability . . . the musical gifts I have . . . the great opportunity to meet new people."

When his performance was over, Patrick and his father were on the stage together. The crowd rose to their feet and cheered for over five minutes.[38]

What a wonderful testimony of the joy of the Lord and how people are drawn to this extraordinary young man. Worshipping the Lord should be a joyful experience, and those around us should see that joy on our faces every day. What favor we would win if our countenance reflected the love of God and the joy of the Lord! Lutheran pastor Craig Harmann wrote:

What would life as a Christian (Lutheran or not)

be like if we smiled more? Yes, this world is harsh, filled with challenges, trials, hatred and many other things. But, why don't we smile? Why can't we smile? Think about it. We are winners! Through Jesus' death and resurrection, we have victory over death and the devil! SMILE!!!! God loves us and provides for us in His own unique, special and perfect way! . . . we HAVE to smile! There are so many reasons for us as Christians to smile. So why don't we? If I had that answer, I'd be a wealthy man . . . . But when we fix our eyes on God, and try to look at things from His per-spective, that love flows through us and out into the world. That is going to be my attempt, and I pray that God works in me and through me to show that love. And the best way to start is by smiling more![39]

Would you like more God-given favor with man? Then unlock that door with a smile. An early Roman, Martial, wrote, "A face that cannot smile is never good."[40]

The world's most famous author, Anonymous, wrote the fol-lowing poem titled, "A Smile":

It costs nothing, but creates much
It enriches those who receive,
Without impoverishing those who give.
It happens in a flash and the memory of it lasts forever.
None are so rich they can get along without it
And none so poor but are richer for its benefits.
It creates happiness in the home,
Fosters good will in a business,

And is the countersign of friends.
It is rest to the weary, daylight to the discouraged,
Sunshine to the sad, and nature's best antidote for trouble.
Yet it cannot be bought, begged, borrowed, or stolen,
For it is something that is no earthly good to anybody
Till it is given away.
If someone is too tired to give you a smile,
Leave one of yours.
For, nobody needs a smile so much
As those who have none to give.[41]

To whom are you drawn—to the one who smiles genuinely, or to the one whose frown drags the ground? Theologian and author Charles Swindoll wrote of joy:

Joy—it makes people wonder at your secret. Yet joy is no secret to the trusting Christian. When we choose to grow closer to God, resting in His character and provision, joy spills over into our lives so that others can't help but notice.

Do you want to be a person of joy? Silly question, isn't it? We would love to live above our circumstances. Or have a great attitude. Or laugh a lot. But joy goes beyond all these things . . . .

Joy becomes a transaction between you and God that others can't help but notice. It's God's life spilling over the brim of your life and into others' lives. When you trust Christ with the details of your life, you experience His life in wonderful excess, and it can't help but give you reason to smile.[42]

When I consider joy, I think of King David, who was so elated to bring the ark of the covenant back to Jerusalem that he danced wholeheartedly before the Lord. He was happy and overwhelmed by gratitude to have the symbol of Jehovah's presence in Jerusalem. Everyone along the route that the ark traveled recognized David's exuberant joy that flowed like a stream from within the king.

While we may not always be happy, we can have joy. What is the difference? Our happiness comes from the outside—situations and circumstances dictate whether or not we are "happy." Joy springs from the well of life, which is internal and never ending. As a Believer, our source of joy comes from our relationship with Jesus Christ. He wants to bless you by giving you favor with man, but you must be prepared to reach out in genuine friendship and exhibit joy from the wellspring He has provided.

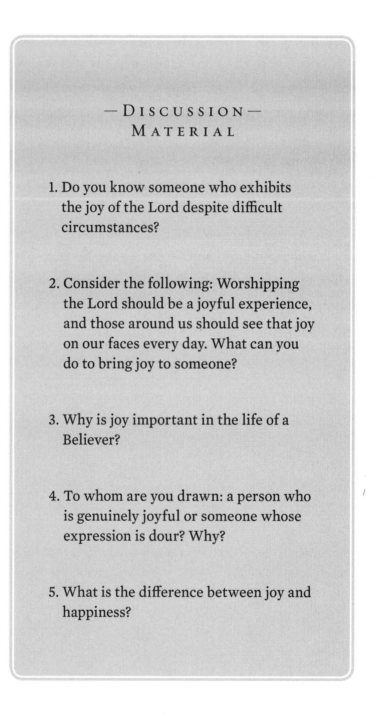

—DISCUSSION—
MATERIAL

1. Do you know someone who exhibits the joy of the Lord despite difficult circumstances?

2. Consider the following: Worshipping the Lord should be a joyful experience, and those around us should see that joy on our faces every day. What can you do to bring joy to someone?

3. Why is joy important in the life of a Believer?

4. To whom are you drawn: a person who is genuinely joyful or someone whose expression is dour? Why?

5. What is the difference between joy and happiness?

— SCRIPTURES ON —
JOY

Rejoicing in hope; patient in tribulation; continuing instant in prayer.

ROMANS 12:12

My brethren, count it all joy when ye fall into divers temptations.

JAMES 1:2

Rejoice in the Lord alway: and again I say, Rejoice.

PHILIPPIANS 4:4

Whom having not seen, ye love; in whom, though now ye see him not, yet believing, ye rejoice with joy unspeakable and full of glory.

1 PETER 1:8

Hitherto have ye asked nothing in my name: ask, and ye shall receive, that your joy may be full.

JOHN 16:24

Now the God of hope fill you with all joy and peace in believing, that ye may abound in hope, through the power of the Holy Ghost.

ROMANS 15:13

For the kingdom of God is not meat and drink; but righteousness, and peace, and joy in the Holy Ghost.

ROMANS 14:17

Therefore my heart is glad, and my glory rejoiceth: my flesh also shall rest in hope.

PSALM 16:9

Rejoice evermore.
1 Thessalonians 5:16

And not only so, but we also joy in God through our
Lord Jesus Christ, by whom we have now received the
atonement.
Romans 5:11

Strengthened with all might, according to his glorious
power, unto all patience and longsuffering with joyfulness.
Colossians 1:11

Thou hast put gladness in my heart, more than in the time
that their corn and their wine increased.
Psalm 4:7

And these things write we unto you, that your joy may be
full.
1 John 1:4

And ye became followers of us, and of the Lord, having
received the word in much affliction, with joy of the Holy
Ghost.
1 Thessalonians 1:6

CHAPTER FOURTEEN

✳

PEACE

. . . and the peace of God, which surpasses all understanding,
will guard your hearts and minds through Christ Jesus.

—PHILIPPIANS 4:7

ONE OF THE THINGS I remember clearly about my encounter with Jesus at age eleven was the enormous sense of peace that flooded my spirit—the calmness He brought into my room that dark and dismal night of my near-death. It not only changed my life; it changed my countenance from one of cringing in fear to one of peace despite the circumstances.

Just as people are drawn to an attitude of joy, so they are drawn to a sense of peacefulness, like iron filings attracted to a magnet. In this turmoil-filled world, people crave the calm. Your countenance can produce a favor-filled life. In his article "The Peace of God," Rev. John F. Barham, pastor of First United Methodist Church in Tavares, Florida, wrote:

> As a truly tranquil person, Jesus lived God's
> Shalom. No matter how difficult the situation Jesus

exuded an inner calm and joy. Jesus was fully present with all—poor & rich, adults & children, leprous & powerful, weak & hopeless . . . He was and is gentle, patient and accepts all . . . Jesus calls us all but not all follow.[43]

This is the kind of peace for which the world is looking and to which it will be drawn. Peace is yet another characteristic that should be exhibited by those to whom God has granted favor with man. As a Believer, when we encounter people it is with a sense of the "peace which surpasses all understanding" (see Philippians 4:7) promised to us by our Lord.

God bestows the blessing of favor with man not just for us to prosper and reap the benefits, but so that we, too, may encourage, uplift, and introduce those in need to the Prince of Peace.

When Jesus met the woman at the well in John chapter 4, verses 28–30, look at her response to Him:

> The woman then left her waterpot, went her way into the city, and said to the men, "Come, see a Man who told me all things that I ever did. Could this be the Christ?" Then they went out of the city and came to Him.

When the peace of God rests upon us, others see His handprint upon our lives, and our influence is felt in their lives. The words of Jesus lodged in the heart of the woman at the well and brought about a transformation.

First Samuel 3:19–20 gives us a picture of how the life of the prophet influenced those around him:

So Samuel grew, and the LORD was with him and let none of his words fall to the ground. And all Israel from Dan to Beersheba knew that Samuel had been established as a prophet of the LORD.

As God gives the Believer favor with those in his/her circle of influence, He will also open hearts to the message of the gospel. As Samuel grew in favor with God and man, his words were not wasted. The picture presented in this verse is one of water–historically a precious commodity in the Middle East–being poured out on rocky ground or an arrow missing its target. Our ultimate aim should be that of living our lives in such a way that our words do not miss their mark.

Second Corinthians 3:2 (MSG) says, "Your very lives are a letter that anyone can read by just looking at you." One of the characteristics of an individual who has found favor with man is a peaceful and joyful countenance.

The world is looking for an elusive peace, longing for it. Peace between countries is often nonexistent; between neighbors, it is fleeting. So-called wars to end all wars didn't. Isaiah prophesied in chapter 9, verse 6:

> For unto us a Child is born,
> Unto us a Son is given;
> And the government will be upon His shoulder.
> And His name will be called
> Wonderful, Counselor, Mighty God,
> Everlasting Father, Prince of Peace.

The night Christ was born in Bethlehem, an angelic host sang,

"Glory to God in the highest, and on earth peace, goodwill toward men!" (Luke 2:14.) For those who have accepted the new birth Jesus offered to all mankind, the peace of God reigns within their hearts. Such is the story of the martyr Polycarp:

A renowned follower of Christ and bishop of Smyrna, Polycarp had become a Christian under the tutelage of John the apostle. Recently, the Roman proconsul [an important magistrate] had been looking for him for days. After arresting and torturing one of Polycarp's servants, they finally learned where he was staying. The soldiers came into the house, but instead of fleeing, Polycarp calmly stated, "God's will be done."

Polycarp asked that food be brought for the soldiers, and he requested an hour for prayer. Amazed by Polycarp's fearlessness, especially for a man his age, the hardened Roman soldiers granted his request. He prayed for two hours for all the Christians he knew and for the universal church, and the soldiers let him.

A proconsul . . . ordered Polycarp to renounce Christ and give obedience to Caesar as Lord. Polycarp answered, "Eighty and six years have I served Christ, nor has He ever done me any harm. How, then, could I blaspheme my King who saved me? You threaten the fire that burns for an hour and then is quenched; but you know not of the fire of the judgment to come, and the fire of eternal punishment. Bring what you will."

Polycarp, the last one of those personally taught by

the apostles, was burned at the stake on . . . February
23, 155.[44]

It is this peace that Isaiah foretold and of which the angels sang.
It is this peace of which the apostle Paul wrote to the church at
Colossae in Colossians 1:19–20:

> For it pleased the Father that in Him all the full-
> ness should dwell, and by Him to reconcile all things
> to Himself, by Him, whether things on earth or things
> in heaven, having made peace through the blood of
> His cross.

It is not a peace that is readily understood by the world. In John
14:25–27, Jesus addressed His disciples on the night before he was to
be taken away from them:

> These things I have spoken to you while being pres-
> ent with you. But the Helper, the Holy Spirit, whom
> the Father will send in My name, He will teach you all
> things, and bring to your remembrance all things that
> I said to you. Peace I leave with you, My peace I give
> to you; not as the world gives do I give to you. Let not
> your heart be troubled, neither let it be afraid.

Rev. John Piper wrote:

> . . . the only kind of heart-peace the world can give
> is peace of mind based on good circumstances. If the
> world can take away our troubles—through health

insurance, or retirement accounts, or flood protec-
tion, or bomb shelters, or labor-saving devices—then
the world can give some peace of mind.[45]

He then said of the kind of peace Jesus wants to bestow on His
followers:

> This is what he [Jesus] is aiming at just before he
> suffers. I want you to have peace. I want you to be
> deeply joyful. I want you to believe in what I say and
> what I do—to have unshakable faith. I want you to
> have the kind of peace that I give, not the world. The
> kind of joy that I give, not the world. The kind of faith,
> I give, not the world. That is the practical outcome of
> these verses—indeed the outcome of this night. This
> suffering. This gospel.[46]

It was the renowned poet Ralph Waldo Emerson who wrote
"What lies behind us and what lies before us are tiny matters com-
pared to what lies within us."[47] What lies within us is the peace Jesus
promised. This was the same Savior who said to the storm that raged
around the disciples on the Sea of Galilee, "Peace!" This is what the
world wants to see in those who believe in Jesus Christ—a calm and
peace that passes all understanding. The characteristic of serenity—
peace—is one that will produce the blessing of God's favor with man.

—Discussion—
Material

1. Read John 4—the story of the woman at the well.

2. Why was she at the well in the middle of the day?

3. What do you think drew her to Jesus?

4. Consider the following: When the peace of God rests upon us, others see His handprint upon our lives, and our influence is felt in their lives.

5. How did the woman respond to Jesus' message?

— SCRIPTURES ON —
PEACE

Blessed are the peacemakers: for they shall be called the children of God.
MATTHEW 5:9

And the peace of God, which passeth all understanding, shall keep your hearts and minds through Christ Jesus.
PHILIPPIANS 4:7

Now the Lord of peace himself give you peace always by all means. The Lord be with you all.
2 THESSALONIANS 3:16

Peace I leave with you, my peace I give unto you: not as the world giveth, give I unto you. Let not your heart be troubled, neither let it be afraid.
JOHN 14:27

Let him eschew evil, and do good; let him seek peace, and ensue it.
1 PETER 3:11

If it be possible, as much as lieth in you, live peaceably with all men.
ROMANS 12:18

Thou wilt keep him in perfect peace, whose mind is stayed on thee: because he trusteth in thee.
ISAIAH 26:3

These things I have spoken unto you, that in me ye might have peace. In the world ye shall have tribulation: but be of good cheer; I have overcome the world.
JOHN 16:33

Follow peace with all men, and holiness, without which no man shall see the Lord.
HEBREWS 12:14

Those things, which ye have both learned, and received, and heard, and seen in me, do: and the God of peace shall be with you.
PHILIPPIANS 4:9

Now the God of hope fill you with all joy and peace in believing, that ye may abound in hope, through the power of the Holy Ghost.
ROMANS 15:13

Deceit is in the heart of them that imagine evil: but to the counsellors of peace is joy.
PROVERBS 12:20

For to be carnally minded is death; but to be spiritually minded is life and peace.
ROMANS 8:6

For God is not the author of confusion, but of peace, as in all churches of the saints.
1 CORINTHIANS 14:33

For the mountains shall depart, and the hills be removed; but my kindness shall not depart from thee, neither shall the covenant of my peace be removed, saith the LORD that hath mercy on thee.
ISAIAH 54:10

✳

CHAPTER FIFTEEN

LONGSUFFERING/ PATIENCE

*We also pray that you will be strengthened
with all his glorious power so you will have all
the endurance and patience you need.*

—COLOSSIANS 1:11 NLT

RICHARD WURMBRAND was a minister of the gospel who had been imprisoned for his stand against Communism. He suffered through years of incarceration and the most brutal of tortures before $7,000 was paid for his ransom. He and his family emigrated to the United States, where he and his wife, Sabina, devoted the remainder of their lives to aiding Christians persecuted for their beliefs.

Before his death in 2001, I was honored to share a meal with Wurmbrand. As we talked that evening, I posed some questions about his experiences in the Communist prison camps. "Did you ever feel as if you were losing your mind?" I asked. He said that he had, but gave those feelings to Christ so he did not have to worry. He also said that when he suffered heartache for his family, he gave those emotions to Christ as well. Finally, he gave his body to Christ and no longer needed to worry about his health. Armed with complete death to his flesh, the Communist prison guards and interrogators no longer had the power to hurt him.

"The guard came for me one day and said, 'You must realize that I can break your arms, your legs, anything I want,'" Wurmbrand told me. "I answered him, 'If you break my arm, I will say, *God loves you* and if you break my leg I will say, *I love you too.*'" He said the stoic guard began to cry at his answer, and Wurmbrand was able to lead him to Christ that day.

Patience in tribulation, the love of Christ, and the joy of the Lord that passes understanding enabled Wurmbrand to gain favor with a prison guard who was, perhaps unknowingly, searching for truth.

Longsuffering is a word too often unused in this modern, "get it now" generation. The inability to secure every want can produce irritation, bias, hypersensitivity, and rage—unfortunately, sometimes even among Believers. Patience is one virtue that genuinely requires God's divine help. I'm reminded of the old cartoon character crying in desperation, "Give me patience, and give it to me NOW!" It is, however, a characteristic that is much needed in reaching people for Christ. In Galatians 5:19–21, the apostle Paul lists what he calls "the works of the flesh":

> Now the works of the flesh are evident, which are: adultery, fornication, uncleanness, lewdness, idolatry, sorcery, hatred, contentions, jealousies, outbursts of wrath, selfish ambitions, dissensions, heresies, envy, murders, drunkenness, revelries, and the like; of which I tell you beforehand, just as I also told you

in time past, that those who practice such things will not inherit the kingdom of God.

Paul could have added, "Neither will they secure the favor of man." So, what is the cure for these vile attributes? He tells us in verses 22–23:

> But the fruit of the Spirit is love, joy, peace, long-suffering, kindness, goodness, faithfulness, gentleness, self-control. Against such there is no law.

These characteristics of the Spirit-filled Believer adorn the child of God. Longsuffering is the fourth on the list, but not lesser in importance, as it speaks of patient endurance. Dr. Charles Stanley, senior pastor of First Baptist Church in Atlanta, Georgia, wrote:

> The Scriptures contain many stories of people who waited years or even decades before the Lord's promises came to pass. What modern believers can learn from the patience of biblical saints like Abraham, Joseph, David, and Paul is that waiting upon the Lord has eternal rewards.[48]

Abraham is a classic example of waiting on Jehovah to do the impossible in providing a son in his old age. God promised a Deliverer after Adam and Eve sinned and were driven from the garden of Eden. Thousands of years passed before the promise was fulfilled in the person of Jesus Christ.

In some verses, the Greek word for longsuffering is *makrothumos—makro* meaning "long" and *thumos*, which translates as "temper—or long-tempered." Have you heard the expressions "short-tempered," "temperamental," "irritable"? Folks with those maladies tend to lose their cool more often than those who possess longsuffering. No one wants to spend time in the presence of someone who reaches the pinnacle of success by tearing others down. Those building blocks resemble the house built of sand that Jesus described in Matthew 7. It is a precarious structure, one where few want to spend time.

Rather than finding favor with man, are you that person who is impatient with clerks, other drivers, your children or spouse? Are you prone to overreact to the simplest situations? Are you tolerated instead of welcomed wholeheartedly? If the answer is yes, check your patience quotient. In Romans 12:14, Paul tells us how we *should* react: "Bless those who persecute you; bless and do not curse."

First Corinthians 13 has come to be known as the "love chapter." It describes the characteristics of a man or woman who puts others first, and in so doing finds favor with man. It is not a calculated behavior, but is instead a love relationship. The apostle wrote in verses 4–7:

> Love suffers long and is kind; love does not envy; love does not parade itself, is not puffed up; does not behave rudely, does not seek its own, is not provoked, thinks no evil; does not rejoice in iniquity, but rejoices in the truth; bears all things, believes all things, hopes all things, endures all things.

Perhaps Paul was building on what Luke wrote in chapter 6, verse 45:

> A good man out of the good treasure of his heart
> brings forth good; and an evil man out of the evil
> treasure of his heart brings forth evil. For out of the
> abundance of the heart his mouth speaks.

What motivates you—love, longsuffering, kindness, regard? Or are you driven by anger, scorn, bias, condescension? Are you more concerned with winning than you are with losing the respect of a colleague, or the opportunity to share the gospel with an unbeliever?

How even the most casual of relationships would change if our lives were governed by longsuffering! Second Corinthians 6:6 (NLT) says:

> We prove ourselves by our purity, our understand-
> ing, our patience, our kindness, by the Holy Spirit
> within us, and by our sincere love.

Our old nature—the old man—can be governed by a very short fuse, too often explosive and troublesome. That is why James admonished in chapter 1, verse 19 that we should be "swift to hear, slow to speak, slow to wrath." Vengeance and retaliation have no place in the life of a Spirit-filled Believer. We must exhibit the same longsuffering to others as that which God has extended to us. Ephesians 4:31–32 says:

> Let all bitterness, wrath, anger, clamor, and evil
> speaking be put away from you, with all malice. And
> be kind to one another, tenderhearted, forgiving one
> another, even as God in Christ forgave you.

Only God can bless us with the favor of man, but you and I can do all within our power to allow the Holy Spirit to develop the characteristics that point the way to Christ—one being longsuffering. As we seek to better know Him, we become more mature in our walk, and the gospel becomes more attractive to those with whom we have daily contact.

—SCRIPTURES ON—
LONGSUFFERING

But the fruit of the Spirit is love, joy, peace, longsuffering, gentleness, goodness, faith.
GALATIANS 5:22

With all lowliness and meekness, with longsuffering, forbearing one another in love.
EPHESIANS 4:2

The Lord is not slack concerning his promise, as some men count slackness; but is longsuffering to us-ward, not willing that any should perish, but that all should come to repentance.
2 PETER 3:9

What if God, willing to shew his wrath, and to make his power known, endured with much longsuffering the vessels of wrath fitted to destruction.
ROMANS 9:22

And the LORD passed by before him, and proclaimed, The LORD, The LORD God, merciful and gracious, longsuffering, and abundant in goodness and truth.
EXODUS 34:6

Or despisest thou the riches of his goodness and forbearance and longsuffering; not knowing that the goodness of God leadeth thee to repentance?
ROMANS 2:4

Rest in the LORD, and wait patiently for him: fret not thyself because of him who prospereth in his way, because of the man who bringeth wicked devices to pass.
PSALM 37:7

But if we hope for that we see not, then do we with patience wait for it.
ROMANS 8:25

But let patience have her perfect work, that ye may be perfect and entire, wanting nothing.
JAMES 1:4

Be careful for nothing; but in every thing by prayer and supplication with thanksgiving let your requests be made known unto God.
PHILIPPIANS 4:6

And patience, experience; and experience, hope.
ROMANS 5:4

Be ye also patient; stablish your hearts: for the coming of the Lord draweth nigh.
JAMES 5:8

Knowing this, that the trying of your faith worketh patience.
JAMES 1:3

Wherefore seeing we also are compassed about with so great a cloud of witnesses, let us lay aside every weight, and the sin which doth so easily beset us, and let us run with patience the race that is set before us.
HEBREWS 12:1

In your patience possess ye your souls.
LUKE 21:19

—DISCUSSION—
MATERIAL

1. Why is patience important in the life of a Believer? How does it attract favor with man?

2. Rather than finding favor with man, are you that person who is impatient with clerks, other drivers, your children or spouse? Are you prone to overreact to the simplest situations? Are you tolerated instead of welcomed wholeheartedly?

3. What motivates you—love, longsuffering, kindness, regard? Or are you driven by anger, scorn, bias, condescension?

4. Are you more concerned with winning than you are with losing the respect of a colleague, or the opportunity to share the gospel with an unbeliever?

5. How would even the most casual of relationships change if our lives were governed by longsuffering?

CHAPTER SIXTEEN

⁂

GENTLENESS

But the fruit of the Spirit is love, joy, peace,
longsuffering, gentleness . . .

—GALATIANS 5:22 KJV

ARE YOU A FRIEND OF SINNERS? What? Of course not! Aren't Believers supposed to draw their robes around them and keep themselves from being tainted by the world? Remember this rhyming ditty: "We don't smoke, and we don't chew, and we don't go with girls [or guys] who do." While it was meant to be humorous, it defined a fundamental belief. But is that really what Jesus did when He walked the earth? No, Jesus knew how to interact with people where they lived—not in ivory towers, but in the streets and alleys of Palestine. The men He called to be His disciples—His daily companions—were a broad cross-section. He chose fishermen, a warrior plotting to overthrow the Romans, a tax collector, and an accountant. What a mismatched group, and yet He gave them favor with man, the ability to learn from Him and then spread the gospel after His ascension.

Jesus shared His message with sinners. When chastised for His choice of friends He responded, "I have come to call not those who think they are righteous, but those who know they are sinners and need to repent" (Luke 5:32 NLT).

In Acts chapter 8, Luke tells the story of an obedient deacon, Philip. His job in the early church was to serve the widows and orphans, yet he was not so deeply engaged in his job that he failed to hear the prompting of the Holy Spirit when ordered to take a detour through the desert. Off in the distance, Philip spots a chariot whose driver is engaged in the dangerous pastime of reading and driving. I'm sure you must have seen that on the freeways around your hometown—a driver who is reading the newspaper or messaging on an iPhone while drinking his/her latte. Philip's order from God was to ride along with the distracted Ethiopian eunuch. Immediately, the deacon recognizes the passage from which the man is reading; it is the book of Isaiah, chapter 53. When Philip asks if the eunuch understands what he is reading, the man admits that he is a seeker in search of the truth. And the deacon is all too happy to provide the needed instruction. Perhaps the eunuch had been fed a steady diet of the Deuteronomy deterrent, which plainly states, "No eunuchs allowed." (See Deuteronomy 23.)

But as the Ethiopian traveler discovers just three chapters later in Isaiah 56:3–5, there is hope for him:

> Do not let the son of the foreigner who has joined himself to the LORD speak, saying, "The LORD has utterly separated me from His people"; nor let the eunuch say, "Here I am, a dry tree." For thus says the LORD: "To the eunuchs who keep My Sabbaths, and choose what pleases Me, and hold fast My covenant, even to them I will give in My house and within My

walls a place and a name better than that of sons and daughters; I will give them an everlasting name that shall not be cut off.

As they journey on down the desert road, Philip gently "opened his mouth, and beginning at this Scripture, preached Jesus to him" (Acts 8:35). What joy for the eunuch—first to learn about the life, death, and resurrection of Jesus Christ, and then to learn that he was eligible to partake of the salvation offered!

When Philip ends his explanation, the Ethiopian is overtaken with joy. He eagerly asks, "See, *here is* water. What hinders me from being baptized?" Then Philip said, "If you believe with all your heart, you may." And he answered and said, "I believe that Jesus Christ is the Son of God" (Acts 8:36–37).

Remember, the two men are plodding down a desert chariot path where there is little water to be found; yet, and perhaps miraculously, water is available for baptism. Rev. Peter Elvin, rector at St. John's Episcopal Church in Williamstown, Massachusetts, wrote of this incident:

> This eunuch . . . will soon be splashing in the waters of new birth and gaining that everlasting name foretold in the 56th chapter of Isaiah and made available to him this day on that wilderness road by God in the present moment. God, who runs alongside us in the breakdown lane, in unlikely characters like Deacon Philip . . . asks to be invited into deep conversation about staying true to the covenant love in which God chooses us.[49]

As Philip listened to the still, small voice that sent him on a missionary journey, so must we. As I was praying one morning in a Jacksonville, Florida, hotel, the Holy Spirit whispered, *"Go eat breakfast now."*

It was early and I wasn't particularly ready to go down to the restaurant, but I've learned not to question that still, small voice. I went. When I walked in, there was only one man seated at a table. Like Philip, who in Acts 8:29 (NIV) was told to "Go to that chariot and stay near it," I was instructed to approach the swarthy gentleman and join him for breakfast.

"May I join you?" I asked as I approached his table. When he nodded, I sat down. "Good morning, how are you? What have you ordered for breakfast?"

When he responded, I said to the waiter, "I'll have the same thing." I then asked about his family. His brow furrowed, and he must have surely thought he knew me because I had sat down with him.

Finally he said with some embarrassment, "I'm so sorry. I seem to have forgotten who you are."

"That's because we've never met."

"What?! We've never met? Then why are we having breakfast together?"

I smiled and replied, "I've been sent here."

He frowned and asked, "By whom? Has someone put out a contract on me?"

"Well, you are partially right; I am a hit man. A Holy Spirit hit man. There *is* a contract out on you." I raised my Bible from my lap and set it on the table. "I've been sent by Jesus Christ."

The man relaxed against the back of his chair and laughed.

"There are nine generations of Greek Orthodox ministers in my genealogy."

I leaned toward him and smiled. "That's not an American Express card to heaven. You can believe the Bible in your head, but until Christ comes into your heart, you're a lost man."

As we talked, I discovered he was discouraged, and I was able to share the gospel of Jesus Christ with him. Then he allowed me to pray with him. It was then that I discovered I was talking to a sports commentator and bookmaker known as Jimmy the Greek.

Some would have shied away from sitting at the same table with a bookie, a gambler. But when you search the Gospels, it is obvious that Jesus dealt daily with people the scribes and Pharisees would have crossed the street to avoid. Jesus came to "preach the gospel to the poor . . . heal the brokenhearted, to proclaim liberty to the captives and recovery of sight to the blind, to set at liberty those who are oppressed; to proclaim the acceptable year of the LORD" (Luke 4:18–19).

God will give us favor with man when approached in the right way. There are those who are born with the natural ability to meet people easily and introduce the plan of salvation into the conversation effortlessly. Others find it difficult to even say hello without blushing and becoming shy. What are some ways we can learn to win friends and influence people for God? We can:

✦ study the Word of God in order to share more effectively;

✦ practice the power of prayer;

✦ learn to be obedient to the Holy Spirit;

✧ develop an awareness for that "still, small voice";

✧ develop your social and conversational skills;

✧ develop ways to disagree without being disagreeable;

✧ learn to get along with others;

✧ be less critical and more caring;

✧ develop the gift of listening sensitively to the needs and desires of others;

✧ hone the art of being genuinely complimentary;

✧ be more positive and less negative.

When we give ourselves over to follow God and His plan for our lives, the natural result is gaining favor with man. In Mark 12:30–31 Jesus gave His followers the key to growing in favor with both God and man:

> "'And you shall love the LORD your God with all your heart, with all your soul, with all your mind, and with all your strength.' This is the first commandment. And the second, like it, is this: 'You shall love your neighbor as yourself.' There is no other commandment greater than these."

If we pursue a life of gentleness with others, favor will be the welcome result. Gentleness is the salve that soothes the burns of life. Those who are gentle, joyful, loving, kind, peaceful, patient, benevolent, compassionate, gracious, and merciful will exhibit characteristics that will attract others.

People flocked to Jesus wherever He went—the city, country, desert, seashore. Why? He lived the attributes of which He taught. The Scriptures tell us that He "had compassion," or He was "moved with compassion." He was a popular dinner guest, even among those with whom He most often disagreed. He treated the hurting, the lost, and the seeking with loving-kindness.

Sadly, gentleness is one characteristic that is too often missing in many relationships, but it is one that draws others to us. Practice the art of gentleness if you wish to find favor with man.

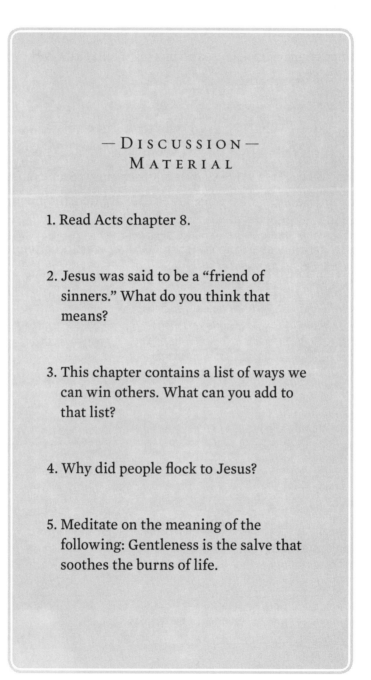

—Discussion—
Material

1. Read Acts chapter 8.

2. Jesus was said to be a "friend of sinners." What do you think that means?

3. This chapter contains a list of ways we can win others. What can you add to that list?

4. Why did people flock to Jesus?

5. Meditate on the meaning of the following: Gentleness is the salve that soothes the burns of life.

—SCRIPTURES ON—
GENTLENESS

To speak evil of no man, to be no brawlers, but gentle, shewing all meekness unto all men.
TITUS 3:2

Thou hast also given me the shield of thy salvation: and thy right hand hath holden me up, and thy gentleness hath made me great.
PSALM 18:35

And the servant of the Lord must not strive; but be gentle unto all men, apt to teach, patient.
2 TIMOTHY 2:24

But the wisdom that is from above is first pure, then peaceable, gentle, and easy to be intreated, full of mercy and good fruits, without partiality, and without hypocrisy.
JAMES 3:17

But the fruit of the Spirit is love, joy, peace, longsuffering, gentleness, goodness, faith.
GALATIANS 5:22

Now I Paul myself beseech you by the meekness and gentleness of Christ, who in presence am base among you, but being absent am bold toward you.
2 CORINTHIANS 10:1

He shall feed his flock like a shepherd: he shall gather the lambs with his arm, and carry them in his bosom, and shall gently lead those that are with young.
ISAIAH 40:11

Thou hast also given me the shield of thy salvation: and thy gentleness hath made me great.
2 SAMUEL 22:36

But we were gentle among you, even as a nurse cherisheth her children.
1 THESSALONIANS 2:7

CHAPTER SEVENTEEN

GOODNESS

*I myself am satisfied about you, my brothers, that
you yourselves are full of goodness, filled with all
knowledge and able to instruct one another.*

—ROMANS 15:14 ESV

PROVERBS 31 GIVES the reader a picture of the virtuous wife—a woman of goodness. Verses 10–12 read:

> Who can find a virtuous wife? For her worth is far
> above rubies. The heart of her husband safely trusts
> her; So he will have no lack of gain.

She does him good and not evil all the days of her life. (Emphasis mine.)

In her book *Beautiful in God's Eyes: The Treasures of the Proverbs 31 Woman*, Christian author Elizabeth George writes:

> . . . with the snapshot of verse 12, we peek right
> into the heart of God's beautiful woman, and we're

startled because it is so clean, so pure, so lovely . . .
No wonder this woman is beautiful in God's eyes! . . .
First of all, as God's beautiful woman, goodness is
part of what God weaves into her character. Doing
good is who she is . . . [50]

When my tour in the army ended, I felt what I can only describe as a force compelling me to a Bible college in Texas to prepare myself for the ministry. Although I had not completed high school, I did have a GED and was certain Bible school was what God intended me to pursue. I was accepted into Southwestern Assemblies of God University in Waxahachie, Texas, and for the next two years spent most nights in the dormitory prayer room wanting desperately to hear His voice again.

It was true that I secretly wrestled with the pain of rejection and abuse from my father. It gnawed at my self-esteem like a trapped rat seeking freedom by chewing on the walls of its prison. It colored every relationship with the deep grays of despondency. There were times I thought I had those feelings under subjection, only to be rocked anew when they resurfaced.

Miraculously, I developed casual friendships at Southwestern, but it was there that I met my own Proverbs 31 woman and very special friend, Carolyn. She had the sweetest smile I'd ever seen. We became best friends and enjoyed that friendship for several years while she was dating others. When Carolyn took me home to meet her parents, I was captivated. It was my first real glimpse of a Christian home filled with love and grace. It was a Sunday morning, and her mom, Peggy, was listening to Christian music while preparing lunch. It was so peaceful in Peggy and Neil's home that I fell in love with Carolyn's parents immediately. I was also soon deeply in love with this special treasure whose name means "joy," and that is just what she brought into my life.

Conversely, there is such evil in the world today, it sounds a bit trite to talk of goodness. And yet, that scripture when given thoughtful consideration is overpowering. It is descriptive of a person of great integrity and moral consistency. It is a picture of a woman who has the best interests of her husband, her family, and her household at heart. Her character is not based on what others think of her, but on what God sees on the inside. American writer and poet Dorothy Parker wrote satirically, "Beauty is only skin deep, but ugly goes clean to the bone."[51]

In 1 Peter 3:3–4, Paul described the very lifeblood of a woman of goodness:

> Do not let your adornment be merely outward—
> arranging the hair, wearing gold, or putting on fine
> apparel—rather let it be the hidden person of the
> heart, with the incorruptible beauty of a gentle and
> quiet spirit, which is very precious in the sight of God.

A godly woman's inner kindness and goodness comes not from her outer wrappings, but from her relationship with her heavenly Father. His love and grace and goodness shine through her as a beacon from a lighthouse guides ships to safe harbor. Peace emanates from within because she knows that she can trust in Jehovah-Machsi—the Lord my Refuge.

When a man or woman allows the Holy Spirit to develop the fruit of the Spirit—the very character of God within them—change is inevitable. Traits such as greediness, malice, disobedience, and unkindness are replaced with love, joy, peace, longsuffering, gentleness, goodness, faith, meekness, and temperance.

The Greek word for "goodness" is *agathosune*. It is a deep-seated goodness that brings with it an inherent honesty and decency, not for the sake of the individual, but toward others. Sometimes that characteristic requires us to speak the truth in love. (See Ephesians 4:15.) We are called upon to challenge someone about a sin that could destroy them. It's not a pleasant thing to do, but even this can be done with kindness and goodness.

Goodness can take the form of giving to aid the needy, helping a sick friend or neighbor, working at the food pantry, and the most difficult, to "pray for those who spitefully use you" (Luke 6:28). Just as we can't force a lemon tree to produce cherries, so we cannot force the development of the fruit of goodness in our own lives. Why? James gave us the answer in chapter 1, verse 17:

> Every good gift and every perfect gift is from above, and comes down from the Father of lights, with whom there is no variation or shadow of turning.

It is this fruit of the Spirit that endears us to others; they are drawn to goodness and kindness. It is a characteristic that will win us favor with man. It is often a simple expression of thanks that can leave the most lasting impression. This story is told of celebrated contralto Marian Anderson:

> After a stirring concert at New York's outdoor Lewissohn Stadium when Marian Anderson had sung encore after encore, a thousand people crowded

around the backstage entrance, asking only a glimpse of the woman who had moved them so deeply.

In response to continued calls, the great singer stepped out onto the porch, still wearing her white concert gown. She stood silent and motionless for a moment, then said quietly to the crowd, "Thank you for letting me sing."[52]

What you may not know about Marian Anderson is that she was raised by devout Christian parents and grew up singing in churches near her home. It was there she developed the kindness that allowed her to be thankful for the opportunity to share her God-given talent.

As Believers, we are called to be salt and light in a dark and decaying world. What does that mean? In the days before iceboxes and then refrigerators were introduced, salt was used as a preservative. Today we know it more as a flavor enhancer to improve the taste of food. If you are not aware of the value of salt, try eliminating it from your diet for a few days. The lack of the proper amount of sodium would soon result in an increased heart rate and dizziness. By sharing the gospel of Jesus Christ with others, you and I become the salt that helps safeguard the world from evil, and through the help of the Holy Spirit, influence it for good. When conflict arises, we are to be mediators; when sorrow overwhelms, we are to be consolers. Where hatred abounds, we are to spread God's love. In Luke 6:35, Jesus says:

> But love your enemies, do good, and lend, hoping for nothing in return; and your reward will be great, and you will be sons of the Most High. For He is kind to the unthankful and evil.

As light in darkness, Jesus said in Matthew 5:14–16:

> You are the light of the world. A city that is set on a hill cannot be hidden. Nor do they light a lamp and put it under a basket, but on a lampstand, and it gives light to all who are in the house. Let your light so shine before men, that they may see your good works and glorify your Father in heaven.

In Carlsbad Caverns, New Mexico, at one point during the tour, the guide asks everyone to sit. The lights are then turned off in the huge underground room for a few moments; the darkness is complete. You literally cannot see your hand held in front of your face. One tiny light can dispel the darkness and bring a sense of security in the depths of darkness. Such is a life of goodness and kindness in the life of an unbeliever.

It is the goodness of Jehovah God that enables us to have favor with man. Our testimony is severely hindered if we lack goodness. Remember the children's song "This Little Light of Mine"?

> This little light of mine, I'm gonna let it shine.
> This little light of mine, I'm gonna let it shine.
> Let it shine, let it shine, let it shine.
> Hide it under a bushel? No! I'm gonna let it shine.
> Hide it under a bushel? No! I'm gonna let it shine.
> Let it shine, let it shine, let it shine.

Goodness and kindness is the light of God that illuminates the lives of others. Goodness brings God-given favor with man. People will then be drawn to you and to the God whom you serve.

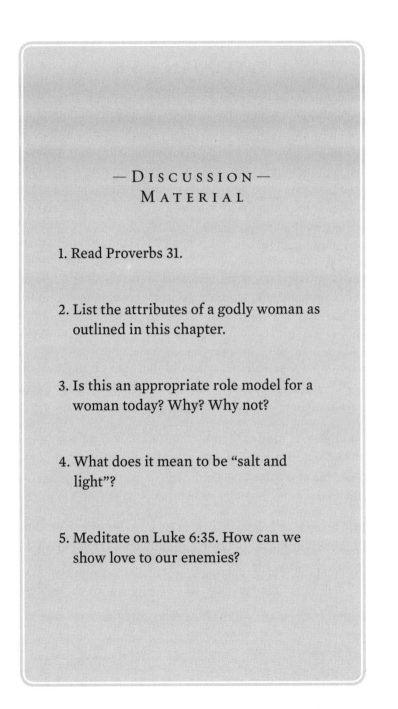

—DISCUSSION—
MATERIAL

1. Read Proverbs 31.

2. List the attributes of a godly woman as outlined in this chapter.

3. Is this an appropriate role model for a woman today? Why? Why not?

4. What does it mean to be "salt and light"?

5. Meditate on Luke 6:35. How can we show love to our enemies?

— SCRIPTURES ON —
GOODNESS

And we know that all things work together for good to them that love God, to them who are the called according to his purpose.
ROMANS 8:28

But the fruit of the Spirit is love, joy, peace, longsuffering, gentleness, goodness, faith.
GALATIANS 5:22

Oh how great is thy goodness, which thou hast laid up for them that fear thee; which thou hast wrought for them that trust in thee before the sons of men!
PSALM 31:19

Surely goodness and mercy shall follow me all the days of my life: and I will dwell in the house of the LORD for ever.
PSALM 23:6

Who is a wise man and endued with knowledge among you? let him shew out of a good conversation his works with meekness of wisdom.
JAMES 3:13

For God so loved the world, that he gave his only begotten Son, that whosoever believeth in him should not perish, but have everlasting life.
JOHN 3:16

Blessed is the man whom thou choosest, and causest to approach unto thee, that he may dwell in thy courts: we shall be satisfied with the goodness of thy house, even of thy holy temple.

PSALM 65:4

And beside this, giving all diligence, add to your faith virtue; and to virtue knowledge.
2 PETER 1:5

This is a faithful saying, and these things I will that thou affirm constantly, that they which have believed in God might be careful to maintain good works. These things are good and profitable unto men.
TITUS 3:8

Let love be without dissimulation. Abhor that which is evil; cleave to that which is good.
ROMANS 12:9

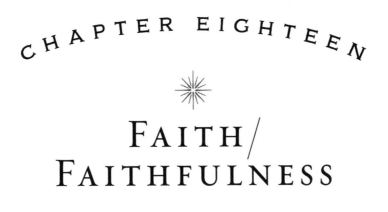

CHAPTER EIGHTEEN

FAITH/ FAITHFULNESS

But the fruit of the Spirit is love, joy, peace,
longsuffering, kindness, goodness, faithfulness . . .

—GALATIANS 5:22

IN THE BOOK *Finding Favor With God*, I wrote of my trip to Beirut in 1983 and the opportunity to witness to the US troops stationed near the airport in that city in Lebanon. The night before the attack on the US Marine barracks, my traveling companions and I spent the night on the beachhead beside the Mediterranean Sea. We were wakened the following morning by the sounds of the terrible blast that claimed the lives of 299 American and French servicemen.

The explosion was so great that the four-story building collapsed in a heap of rubble. Many of the dead had not been killed by the blast itself, but were crushed beneath the cinder-block building as it pancaked in on itself.

My dear friend Dr. James Dobson wrote of that tragic day in his book *Children at Risk*:

> One of the most tragic events during the Reagan Presidency was the Sunday morning terrorist bombing of the Marine barracks in Beirut, in which hundreds of Americans were killed or wounded as they slept. Many of us can still recall the terrible scenes as the dazed survivors worked to dig out their trapped brothers from beneath the rubble.

A few days after the tragedy, I recall coming across an extraordinary story. Marine Corps Commandant Paul X Kelly, visited some of the wounded survivors then in a Frankfurt, Germany, hospital. Among them was Corporal Jeffrey Lee Nashton, severely wounded in the incident. Nashton had so many tubes running in and out of his body that a witness said he looked more like a machine than a man; yet he survived.

As Kelly neared him, Nashton, struggling to move and racked with pain, motioned for a piece of paper and a pen. He wrote a brief note and passed it back to the Commandant. On the slip of paper were but two words—"Semper Fi" the Latin motto of the Marines meaning "forever faithful." With those two simple words Nashton spoke for the millions of Americans who have sacrificed body and limb and their lives for their country—those who have remained faithful.[53]

I love the definition of faithfulness offered by Pastor Jimmy Dean of First Baptist Church in Barberville, Florida:

"Faithfulness is love hanging on." It is love saying, "I will not quit. There may be misunderstandings, there may be disappointments, there may be discouragements, but I will not quit. . . . Even though there is discouragement & disappointment, I will not let go, I will not quit . . . because God has called me to be faithful."[54]

As Believers, we are called to be faithful—trustworthy—in all that has been committed to us, whether it is our relationship with Christ, our marriage, our children, or our employer. With the practice of faithfulness one must include dependability, commitment, diligence, persistence, loyalty, and devotion. These are characteristics a spouse seeks in a mate, an employer in an employee, and a friend in a companion. The apostle Paul called Tychicus a "beloved brother, faithful minister in the Lord" (see Colossians 4:7). He referred to Epaphras as a "faithful minister of Christ" (see Colossians 1:7). The apostle also called Onesimus a "faithful and beloved brother" (see Colossians 4:9) and, along with Timothy, called him "son." (See Philemon 1:10 and 1 Timothy 1:2.) These colaborers had earned the respect not only of Paul, but of those alongside whom they worked.

One woman who exemplifies faithfulness is a Bible character of whom I've written several times—Ruth. This sweet-natured lady was not afraid of hard work. Like the Proverbs 31 woman, Ruth rose while it was yet night and provided food (see verse 15) for her and Naomi, her mother-in-law. Her faithfulness won favor with Boaz, led to their marriage, and gained Ruth a place in the genealogy of Jesus.

This was not a coincidence, but the powerful hand of a loving Jehovah-Jireh who made provision for Ruth. It was the Holy Spirit who whispered into the ear of Boaz, *"See that lovely and diligent young woman. Provide for her."* His obedience had kingdom consequences for a young woman who was just going about the business of taking care of a loved one, following the path God had laid out for her.

Like Ruth, you and I are not meant to see the completed tapestry, but we can make a difference by being faithful to the work of God. It is He who will grant us favor with man as we become good and faithful servants. What does that involve?

✧ For a loving father, it is getting up and going off to work to provide for his household.

✧ For a gentle mother, it is wiping runny noses and mopping up spilled milk.

✧ For a pastor, it is serving his congregation in untold ways.

And God provides relief in just as many ways:

✧ For the brokenhearted, it is trusting in your heavenly Father to give you hope.

✧ For the suffering, it is reaching out to the One who can bind your wounds.

✧ For the sinner, it is grace.

Every act of faithfulness, no matter how small, has the capacity to touch the life of someone. As God bestows upon you favor with man, your trustworthiness can be used in a myriad of ways to bring glory to God.

Faithfulness equals obedience: simply doing what God's Word and the Holy Spirit instruct us to do. It is, again, listening to that still, small voice and responding. It is time spent in the Word and in prayer. Jesus said in John 10:14, "I am the good shepherd; and I know My *sheep,* and am known by My own." And in verse 27, "My sheep hear My voice, and I know them, and they follow Me." The old adage "Practice makes perfect" is valid. The more time we spend with Jesus, the better able we are to recognize His voice and respond to Him.

Just as faithfulness is a characteristic of a Believer, so are there other attributes to being faithful. Proverbs 27:6 (NLT) says, "Wounds from a sincere friend are better than many kisses from an enemy." Friends sometimes have to speak the truth lovingly for our greater good. The colleague who can faithfully, honestly and kindly offer constructive criticism is a friend, indeed. That man or woman has earned our loyalty.

God has called us to faithfulness and that includes trusting Him absolutely, even when conditions indicate otherwise. Lamentations 3:22–23 (NIV) says, "Because of the LORD's great love we are not consumed, for his compassions never fail. They are new every morning; great is your faithfulness."

And in 1 Corinthians 1:9 (NIV), Paul wrote, "God is faithful, who has called you into fellowship with his Son, Jesus Christ our Lord." Faithfulness should be the response to our faithful heavenly Father. You and I have not been called to success according to the world's standards, but according to God's. In Micah 6:8, the prophet sets forth man's responsibility:

He has shown you, O man, what *is* good; And what does the LORD require of you but to do justly, to love mercy, and to walk humbly with your God?

God has called us to be responsible stewards of all with which He has entrusted us. In Luke 16:1–13, Jesus tells His disciples the parable of the "Unjust Steward." It has been called a character study with emphasis on how God sees our actions. One important lesson to be learned from this passage is that of trustworthiness. In verse 10, we read, "He who is faithful in what is least is faithful also in much."

There is an account in 2 Samuel 21:8–14 that is not often the subject of a Sunday sermon; perhaps it should be, because it is a tribute to faithfulness and loyalty:

> So the king took Armoni and Mephibosheth [not Jonathan's son], the two sons of Rizpah the daughter of Aiah, whom she bore to Saul, and the five sons of Michal the daughter of Saul, whom she brought up for Adriel the son of Barzillai the Meholathite; and he delivered them into the hands of the Gibeonites, and they hanged them on the hill before the LORD. So they fell, all seven together, and were put to death in the days of harvest, in the first days, in the beginning of barley harvest. Now Rizpah the daughter of Aiah took sackcloth and spread it for herself on the rock, from the beginning of harvest until the late rains poured on them from heaven. And she did not allow the birds of the air to rest on them by day nor the beasts of the field by night. And David was told

what Rizpah the daughter of Aiah, the concubine of Saul, had done. Then David went and took the bones of Saul, and the bones of Jonathan his son, from the men of Jabesh Gilead who had stolen them from the street of Beth Shan, where the Philistines had hung them up, after the Philistines had struck down Saul in Gilboa. So he brought up the bones of Saul and the bones of Jonathan his son from there; and they gathered the bones of those who had been hanged. They buried the bones of Saul and Jonathan his son in the country of Benjamin in Zelah, in the tomb of Kish his father.

Rizpah, like so many women throughout history, was a victim of conflict—of rivalry and hostilities between two warring peoples. Embroiled in the war that so directly affected Rizpah were the Gibeonites, a people Joshua had sworn an oath not to destroy (see Joshua 9). When he was anointed king, however, Saul set out to destroy the people with whom Joshua had a covenant. Once Saul had been slain on Mount Gilboa, the Gibeonites approached David and sought to be compensated for Saul's flagrant violation of Joshua's oath. David delayed in responding to their demands, and as a result, severe famine gripped Israel. As deprivation pervaded the land, David inquired of the Lord for the cause of the famine. God responded to the king's pleas:

And the LORD answered, "It is because of Saul and his bloodthirsty house, because he killed the Gibeonites" (2 Samuel 21:1).

The response of the Gibeonite king in verses 5–6 left David bereft, but obligated:

> Then they answered the king, "As for the man who consumed us and plotted against us, that we should be destroyed from remaining in any of the territories of Israel, let seven men of his descendants be delivered to us, and we will hang them before the LORD in Gibeah of Saul, whom the LORD chose."

Seven of Saul's offspring, including the two sons of Rizpah, were brutally butchered by the Gibeonites, not to assuage God's demands, but to quench the bloody thirst for retribution. All too often, the innocent suffer for the brutality of their leaders.

In verse 10, we glimpse a mother whose grief extends not only to her children, but to their half-brothers—a love as "strong as death" (Song of Solomon 8:6). What a horrific sight that met those who had gone out to gather the barley harvest—seven men hanging between heaven and earth in various states of decay. Standing on a rock nearby was a woman wrapped in sackcloth—which symbolized humiliation—brandishing a weapon skyward to ward off the birds of prey that circled overhead, "And she did not allow the birds of the air to rest on them by day nor the beasts of the field by night" (v. 10b). She stood vigil, her love giving her no rest "from the beginning of harvest until the late rains poured on them from heaven" (v. 10a).

The revenge of the Gibeonites was not Jehovah sanctioned—for the law clearly stated in Deuteronomy 21:22–23:

> If a man has committed a sin deserving of death, and he is put to death, and you hang him on a tree, his

body shall not remain overnight on the tree, but you shall surely bury him that day . . .

One commentator wrote:

> Rizpah continued watching the mouldering bodies of the dead standing out stark against the sky. Her beautiful, sacrificial motherhood wrestled through anxious days and more anxious nights with the foul stench of those rotting corpses filling her nostrils. Here is an episode unmatched in literature.[55]

Rizpah defended the bodies of the dead till the rains finally came—a token that God had withdrawn His judgment. Water out of the heavens, reviving the famine-stricken land, was recognized as the sign of God's mercy, and that the painful watch in sackcloth on the dead was over. "Refrain . . . your eyes from tears; . . . your work shall be rewarded . . . they shall come back from the land of the enemy" (Jeremiah 31:16).

King David was advised of Rizpah's solemn vigil, of her faithfulness to Saul's slaughtered sons, and ordered the corpses to be taken down. He also instructed that the bones of Saul and Jonathan be recovered from Beth-shan and buried with those of his seven other sons.

Rizpah's loyalty and determination won her favor with man, and not just any man, but the king of Israel. If we wish favor with man, the key is being trustworthy, faithful to do what we say we will do—when we say we will do it. It's part of the "do unto others" in Luke 6:31. People gravitate toward those who are faithful, loyal, and reliable.

—DISCUSSION—
MATERIAL

1. Read 2 Samuel 21.

2. Faithfulness has been described as "love hanging on." How does that apply to Rizpah?

3. What does it mean to be faithful?

4. Name several others in the Bible who were called "faithful."

5. How did Rizpah's faithfulness win her favor with man?

— SCRIPTURES ON —

Faith

For by grace are ye saved through faith; and that not of yourselves: it is the gift of God.

EPHESIANS 2:8

(For we walk by faith, not by sight.)

2 CORINTHIANS 5:7

But without faith it is impossible to please him: for he that cometh to God must believe that he is, and that he is a rewarder of them that diligently seek him.

HEBREWS 11:6

For whatsoever is born of God overcometh the world: and this is the victory that overcometh the world, even our faith.

1 JOHN 5:4

And the Lord said, If ye had faith as a grain of mustard seed, ye might say unto this sycamine tree, Be thou plucked up by the root, and be thou planted in the sea; and it should obey you.

LUKE 17:6

Now faith is the substance of things hoped for, the evidence of things not seen.

HEBREWS 11:1

But Jesus turned him about, and when he saw her, he said, Daughter, be of good comfort; thy faith hath made thee whole. And the woman was made whole from that hour.

MATTHEW 9:22

For by grace are ye saved through faith; and that not of yourselves: it is the gift of God.
EPHESIANS 2:8

Blessed is that man that maketh the LORD his trust, and respecteth not the proud, nor such as turn aside to lies.
PSALM 40:4

Knowing this, that the trying of your faith worketh patience.
JAMES 1:3

And he said to the woman, Thy faith hath saved thee; go in peace.
LUKE 7:50

Then touched he their eyes, saying, According to your faith be it unto you.
MATTHEW 9:29

Ye see then how that by works a man is justified, and not by faith only.
JAMES 2:24

And Jesus answering saith unto them, Have faith in God.
MARK 11:22

Above all, taking the shield of faith, wherewith ye shall be able to quench all the fiery darts of the wicked.
EPHESIANS 6:16

CHAPTER NINETEEN

MEEKNESS

Take My yoke upon you and learn from Me,
for I am gentle and lowly in heart,
and you will find rest for your souls.

—MATTHEW 11:29

TOO OFTEN WE ASSOCIATE meekness with weakness, and nothing could be further from the truth. While our Lord was said to be gentle, He exhibited great strength. Meekness is not weakness, but rather great power under control. There is a blessing to be found in the life of a truly meek Believer, for "The meek will he guide in judgment: and the meek will he teach his way" (Psalm 25:9 KJV).

Pastor and author John Piper wrote, "Meekness is the power to absorb adversity and criticism without lashing back."[56] The world deals daily with those who lash out when mistreated in some way. The truly meek Christian has the ability not to retaliate when wronged. James cautioned us how to respond when ill-treated. He wrote in chapter 1, verses 19–21:

So then, my beloved brethren, let every man be swift to hear, slow to speak, slow to wrath; for the wrath of man does not produce the righteousness of God. Therefore lay aside all filthiness and overflow of wickedness, and receive with meekness the implanted word, which is able to save your souls.

He adds the real zinger in verse 26:

If anyone among you thinks he is religious, and does not bridle his tongue but deceives his own heart, this one's religion is useless.

Can meekness bring true favor with man, or does it leave us open to abuse and maltreatment? The truly meek person is "eager to listen and learn." When challenged, he doesn't jump in with both feet and whip the other individual into shape. If we wish to mirror the way Jesus treated people, we will treat others with gentleness, respect, and humility. This is in total contrast to the way the Enemy would plot to have us respond—with anger, belligerence, and violence—and thus alienate the very people we wish to reach with the message of the gospel.

In today's ego-fed, self-centered world, meekness is a trait too often lost. Temperamental people rage uncontrollably while others are trodden underfoot. Few people want to be known as being meek. Even when we wear bracelets or caps emblazoned with the sentiment, "What would Jesus do?" meekness is a lost art among some Believers. This despite the fact that in Matthew 11:29 (KJV), Jesus said, "Take my yoke upon you, and learn of me; for I am meek and lowly in heart: and ye shall find rest unto your souls."

When was the last time you told someone you were meek, even though it is a fruit of the Spirit? Meekness should be a much-sought-after character trait, especially if we want to be true disciples of Christ. Why is it not? Have you checked a Thesaurus for synonyms of *meek*? You will find words such as *timid, submissive, docile, weak, cowed, fearful, compliant,* and *mild.* These are not descriptive words with which today's macho society wants to be linked. But can you honestly say that these words are descriptive of Jesus, or Moses, or Elijah, or Paul—each of whom was unafraid to confront evil? After all, it was Jesus who called the religionists of His day "whitewashed tombs—beautiful outwardly, but inside are full of dead men's bones and all uncleanness" (see Matthew 23:27).

The leadership authority of Moses was challenged by Korah, Dathan, and Abiram in Numbers 16. Rather than packing his tent and returning to his father-in-law Jethro's abode, Moses faced his adversaries. In verses 28–33, Moses stood his ground confidently knowing that Jehovah stood with him:

> And Moses said: "By this you shall know that the LORD has sent me to do all these works, for I have not done them of my own will. If these men die naturally like all men, or if they are visited by the common fate of all men, then the LORD has not sent me. But if the LORD creates a new thing, and the earth opens its mouth and swallows them up with all that belongs to them, and they go down alive into the pit, then you will understand that these men have rejected the LORD."
>
> Now it came to pass, as he finished speaking all these words, that the ground split apart under them,

and the earth opened its mouth and swallowed them up, with their households and all the men with Korah, with all their goods. So they and all those with them went down alive into the pit; the earth closed over them, and they perished from among the assembly.

Those are not the words of men meek and mild, but of men who knew their God and were unafraid to trust Him to meet their needs. When Jesus delivered His treatise we call the "Sermon on the Mount" in Matthew 5, He included this character trait as number three on His list in verse 5, "Blessed *are* the meek, for they shall inherit the earth."

According to John Piper, meekness "does mean that we don't have hair-triggers. It does mean that our disposition is one of readiness to listen and learn. It does mean that we are slow to write a person off, slow to condemn, slow to anger."[57]

The world around us is an angry place. Political columnist Peter Stern wrote in 2011 in "Politics and the Universe":

If the U.S. economy is falling apart there is no hope for the rest of the world. In the United Kingdom there has been unrest, protesting and looting. The political climate in the Mid-East (Syria, Egypt, Yemen, etc.) is a hot-bed of violence. It seems that chaos is spreading around the globe. Few places are immune to joblessness, hunger, oppression, anger and violence.[58]

Jesus said in John 16:33 (NIV):

> I have told you these things, so that in me you may
> have peace. In this world you will have trouble. But
> take heart! I have overcome the world.

People are looking for those who can point the way to hope amidst the unrest; not those who stand in the town square and preach civil rebellion and warfare, but those who know the Prince of Peace on a personal basis.

Pastor and author A. W. Tozer once wrote:

> The meek man is not a human mouse afflicted with
> a sense of his own inferiority. Rather he may be in his
> moral life as bold as a lion and as strong as Samson;
> but he has stopped being fooled about himself. He has
> accepted God's estimate of his own life. He knows he
> is as weak and helpless as God declared him to be, but
> paradoxically, he knows at the same time that he is
> in the sight of God of more importance than angels.
> In himself, nothing; in God, everything. That is his
> motto.[59]

When taken at face value, verse 5 of Matthew 5 seems to go against the grain. How can those who are meek—remember the world's definition of weak—inherit the earth? Our friend Anonymous said:

> Life is a competition. Survival of the fittest, fight
> for what you want or someone else will take it.[60]

That is the general consensus in today's climate. Instead of accepting God's Word as truth, all too often Believers take on the world's mantra: If you want it, take it! Rather than being conformed to the image of His Son (see Romans 8:29), we become conformed to the world. But Paul wrote in Romans 12:2 that we should "be transformed by the renewing of your mind, that you may prove what *is* that good and acceptable and perfect will of God."

How will you respond? The decision is yours: Will you adhere to the Word and gladly follow Jesus' direction? Will you learn from His teachings and grow in grace and favor with God and man, or will you follow the dictates of the world?

Before you answer that question, let's look more in-depth at the actual meaning of the word *meekness*. It has been loosely translated as *humility* and/or *gentleness*—words that do not precisely account for the actual meaning. In *The Complete Word Study Dictionary: New Testament*, editor Dr. Spiros Zodhiates introduces the word *prautes* and gives us a beautiful definition of *meek*: He writes:

> *Prautes*, according to Aristotle, is the middle standing between two extremes, getting angry without reason, and not getting angry at all. Therefore, *prautes* is getting angry at the right time, in the right measure, and for the right reason.... [I]t is a condition of mind and heart which demonstrates gentleness, not in weakness, but in power. It is a balance born in strength of character.[61]

Meekness and a self-inflated ego cannot march hand in hand to the beat of God's drummer. In Romans 12:3 (NLT), Paul addressed the egotistical Believer when he said:

Don't think you are better than you really are. Be honest in your evaluation of yourselves, measuring yourselves by the faith God has given us.

Jesus preceded "blessed are the meek" with "blessed are the poor in spirit," which indicates that we are to approach God with a deep sense of contrition and a tender conscience—a godly sorrow that leads to repentance. (See 2 Corinthians 7:10.) This produces Believers who are saved, justified, sanctified, and freed from the penalty of sin. It is in this state that God can develop a true sense of meekness in His child.

Writer Carolyn Arends in an article titled, "Strength in Meekness: What to do with the anger that saps strength," wrote:

> If meekness isn't weakness, what is it? The word has an association with domesticated animals, specifically beasts of burden. At first blush, this etymology doesn't thrill me; I don't particularly aspire to be ox-like. But when I think about it, an ox at the plow is not weak but extraordinarily strong. The key, though, is that his power is harnessed and directed. Perhaps meekness is strength that is submitted to an appropriate authority.[62]

It is this God-infused type of meekness that will produce favor with man, but it is a characteristic that is sadly lacking today.

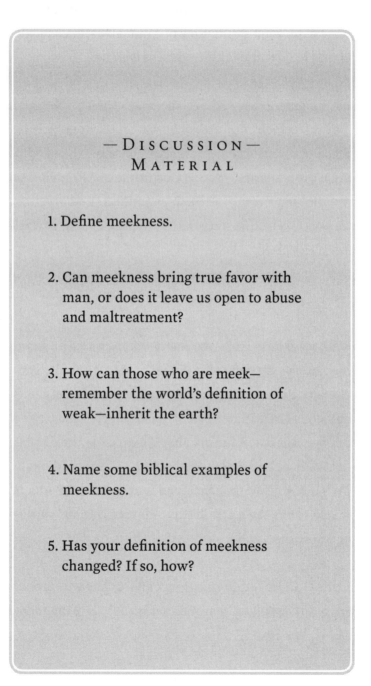

—DISCUSSION—
MATERIAL

1. Define meekness.

2. Can meekness bring true favor with man, or does it leave us open to abuse and maltreatment?

3. How can those who are meek—remember the world's definition of weak—inherit the earth?

4. Name some biblical examples of meekness.

5. Has your definition of meekness changed? If so, how?

— SCRIPTURES ON —
MEEKNESS

To speak evil of no man, to be no brawlers, but gentle, shewing all meekness unto all men.
TITUS 3:2

Blessed are the meek: for they shall inherit the earth.
MATTHEW 5:5

Take my yoke upon you, and learn of me; for I am meek and lowly in heart: and ye shall find rest unto your souls.
MATTHEW 11:29

The meek will he guide in judgment: and the meek will he teach his way.
PSALM 25:9

But let it be the hidden man of the heart, in that which is not corruptible, even the ornament of a meek and quiet spirit, which is in the sight of God of great price.
1 PETER 3:4

But the meek shall inherit the earth; and shall delight themselves in the abundance of peace.
PSALM 37:11

But sanctify the Lord God in your hearts: and be ready always to give an answer to every man that asketh you a reason of the hope that is in you with meekness and fear.
1 PETER 3:15

Who is a wise man and endued with knowledge among you? let him shew out of a good conversation his works with meekness of wisdom.
JAMES 3:13

(Now the man Moses was very meek, above all the men which were upon the face of the earth.)
NUMBERS 12:3

Wherefore lay apart all filthiness and superfluity of naughtiness, and receive with meekness the engrafted word, which is able to save your souls.
JAMES 1:21

Brethren, if a man be overtaken in a fault, ye which are spiritual, restore such an one in the spirit of meekness; considering thyself, lest thou also be tempted.
GALATIANS 6:1

With all lowliness and meekness, with longsuffering, forbearing one another in love.
EPHESIANS 4:2

Put on therefore, as the elect of God, holy and beloved, bowels of mercies, kindness, humbleness of mind, meekness, longsuffering.
COLOSSIANS 3:12

Seek ye the LORD, all ye meek of the earth, which have wrought his judgment; seek righteousness, seek meekness: it may be ye shall be hid in the day of the LORD's anger.
ZEPHANIAH 2:3

In meekness instructing those that oppose themselves; if God peradventure will give them repentance to the acknowledging of the truth.
2 TIMOTHY 2:25

CHAPTER TWENTY

TEMPERANCE/
SELF-CONTROL

*A man without self-control is like a city
broken into and left without walls.*

—PROVERBS 25:28 ESV

IT WAS NOT THE APOSTLE PAUL or one of the writers of the Gospels who said, "Educate your children to self-control, to the habit of holding passion and prejudice and evil tendencies subject to an upright and reasoning will, and you have done much to abolish misery from their future and crimes from society," it was Benjamin Franklin.[63]

Manoah and his wife were diligent in raising their son Samson to be a "Nazarite," as instructed by an angel of the Lord before Samson was born. The vow required the individual to:

> Abstain from wine, wine vinegar, grapes, raisins, intoxicating liquors, vinegar distilled from such substances, and eating or drinking any substance that contains any trace of grapes. [Numbers 6:3–4]

> Refrain from cutting the hair on one's head; but to allow the locks of the head's hair to grow. [Numbers 6:5]

> Not to become ritually impure by contact with corpses or graves, even those of family members. [Numbers 6:6–7][64]

Temperance was not one of the top ten things to teach their son. At his birth, Samson was dedicated to Jehovah and as a young man took his Nazarite vows very seriously. The power of God rested upon him to the point that at one time he killed a young lion with nothing but his bare hands (see Judges 14:5–6). On another occasion he was bound and delivered to the Philistines. He ripped the bonds asunder, grabbed the jawbone of an ass, and killed 1,000 of the enemy (see Judges 15:14–16). He was no ordinary man. Despite his great strength, he failed to exhibit self-control. His life was in constant emotional upheaval between lust and anger. He was tossed from judge to profligate, back to judge; from the leader of God's people to follower of a Philistine prostitute.

In Judges 16, we read the story of Samson's downfall at the hands of Delilah. Although we read in other passages that the Israelite judge was tempted by harlots, and especially those in Philistia, Delilah is not referred to as a harlot. Was she a woman of the night, a wealthy widow, or just someone who could be bribed by the lure of money? Whatever her motivation, she agreed to entice Samson to reveal the secret of his strength. Judges 16:4 reveals that Samson loved Delilah—but it makes no claim of any reciprocity on her part. She seems to have been induced only by monetary gain.

Taking advantage of her lover's lack of self-control and her own powers of persuasion and seduction, Delilah preened and pouted her way into Samson's confidence. Oh, Samson toyed with her a bit before actually revealing the secret of his strength, but bare his soul he finally did. Samson divulged that he had been set apart at birth for service to God. He had taken a vow never to cut his hair, the outward sign of his covenant with Jehovah.

Luring Samson into taking a nap on her lap, Delilah called for her Philistine collaborators, who rushed in, bound the strongman, and shaved off his locks. Unable to defend himself, Samson was taken captive. His eyes were gouged out and he was imprisoned in Gaza, where he was forced to undergo severe punishment. His lack of self-control had cost him dearly. He found himself bound and alone. Paul wrote in Romans 8:12–13a:

> Therefore, brethren, we are debtors—not to the flesh, to live according to the flesh. For if you live according to the flesh you will die . . .

This was the roller coaster on which Samson found himself and why he awoke one morning only to discover "that the LORD had departed from him (see Judges 16:20).

But something began to happen inside Samson even as his hair grew. He realized his need for Jehovah. In his humility, he prayed to Jehovah-Tsori—the Lord my Strength—and God answered. As the Philistines gathered to honor their false god Dagon, some of the leaders called for Samson to be paraded before the people to further humiliate him. Judges 16:25b–30 tells the rest of the story:

> So they called for Samson from the prison, and he performed for them. And they stationed him between the pillars. Then Samson said to the lad who held

him by the hand, "Let me feel the pillars which support the temple, so that I can lean on them." Now the temple was full of men and women. All the lords of the Philistines were there—about three thousand men and women on the roof watching while Samson performed. Then Samson called to the LORD, saying, "O Lord GOD, remember me, I pray! Strengthen me, I pray, just this once, O God, that I may with one blow take vengeance on the Philistines for my two eyes!" And Samson took hold of the two middle pillars which supported the temple, and he braced himself against them, one on his right and the other on his left. Then Samson said, "Let me die with the Philistines!" And he pushed with all his might, and the temple fell on the lords and all the people who were in it. So the dead that he killed at his death were more than he had killed in his life.

Samson is one of countless individuals then and now who have suffered because of the lack of self-control—witness the alcoholic, gambler, drug addict, an individual captivated by pornography, or someone unable to control anger. There are as many ways to relinquish self-control as there are individuals tempted to do so.

Just as lack of self-control ultimately cost Samson his life, so it can happen to the most unassuming man or woman. Consider the case of two women in Alabama—one now dead and the other convicted of manslaughter:

The two drivers had been battling for about four miles, jousting for position in the heavy rush-hour traffic streaming homeward from Birmingham along southbound Interstate 65. After one vehicle cut off the other one, they played a cat-and-mouse game, tailgating, lane-changing, slamming on brakes until they got off at the same exit.

Gena Foster, 34, was racing to pick up her daughter Francie, a 4-year-old with a mop of blond hair, at an after-school program for children with cerebral palsy. Shirley Henson, 40, was on her way home to her husband and dogs in a quiet cul de sac. But when the two cars came to a stop at a traffic light on the darkened exit ramp, Foster jumped out and started toward the immaculate black sport-utility vehicle idling behind her.

Inside the Toyota 4-Runner, Henson reached into the console next to the seat, where she kept a .38-caliber revolver and a cell phone. As Foster approached her door, Henson lowered the window about halfway and reached for the revolver. She fired a single shot, striking Foster in the left cheek. Foster crumpled to the pavement, blood gushing from her face, dying. She never made it to school.[65]

After her trial, Henson was sentenced to thirteen years in a correctional facility; she served four years and two months. Her life was forever changed by an act of road rage, a loss of self-control.

The scripture from Proverbs 25:28 gives a picture of a defenseless city whose walls had been broken down. A person with no self-control is an easy prey to compulsions. President Harry S Truman said:

> In reading the lives of great men, I found that the first victory they won was over themselves . . . self-discipline with all of them came first.[66]

Inviting God to grow the fruit of the Spirit in your life is an excellent means of growing in favor with God and man. We only have to go back to the Old Testament scriptures detailing the Ten Commandments to learn how to treat others. The entire passage can be condensed into ten words: first do others no harm—either by word or deed.

Then look at the Sermon on the Mount and read how our Lord taught us to conduct ourselves. Jesus taught that those in whom the Holy Spirit is developing love, joy, peace, longsuffering, kindness, goodness, faithfulness, gentleness, self-control are those who grow in favor with man. Why? There may be some in the world who are so malevolent, so vile, that they actually abhor the good. Many, however, are drawn to the godly characteristics outlined in the Word.

Favor with man is a by-product of favor with God. Allen Randolph, pastor of Trinity Church in San Antonio, wrote:

> Favor can do what your best skills and efforts may not—opening doors otherwise closed to you, removing obstacles impeding your progress, introducing unanticipated opportunities, and inviting you into select circles and relationships. **Favor is networking in the best possible way!** Pray for favor; walk before God in integrity and obedience; extend favor to others; anticipate favor from others. Here is God's Word for you everyday, *"Now is the time of God's favor, now is the day of salvation!"* 2 Corinthians 6:2 NIV.[67]

In *Seasons of Life*, Dr. Charles Swindoll wrote of self-control:

Self-control, another word for restraint, is honored by the Lord as the "anchor virtue" on His relay team that runs life's race for His glory . . . . When we are angered, God instructs to restrain ourselves . . . When we are prompted to talk too much, He says, "Hold it! Better keep that to yourself!" . . . When food is stacked before us, God is pleased when we restrain ourselves from gluttony . . . . When money is to be earned, spent, saved, or invested, the use of restraint is the order of the day . . . . Removing restraints from your life may seem like an exciting adventure, but it inevitably leads to tragedy . . . Take away the brakes and your life, like your car, is transformed into an unguided missile—destined for disaster.[68]

The key to favor with man is found in Proverbs 3:3–4:

Let not mercy and truth forsake you; bind them around your neck, write them on the tablet of your heart, and so find favor and high esteem in the sight of God and man.

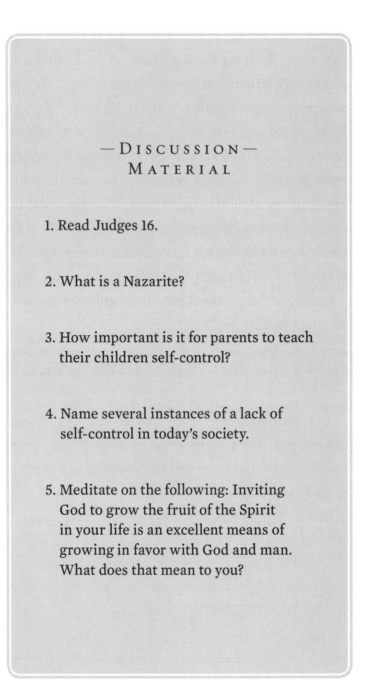

—DISCUSSION—
MATERIAL

1. Read Judges 16.

2. What is a Nazarite?

3. How important is it for parents to teach their children self-control?

4. Name several instances of a lack of self-control in today's society.

5. Meditate on the following: Inviting God to grow the fruit of the Spirit in your life is an excellent means of growing in favor with God and man. What does that mean to you?

— SCRIPTURES ON —
TEMPERANCE/
SELF-CONTROL

Teaching us that, denying ungodliness and worldly lusts, we should live soberly, righteously, and godly, in this present world.

TITUS 2:12

But I keep under my body, and bring it into subjection: lest that by any means, when I have preached to others, I myself should be a castaway.

1 CORINTHIANS 9:27

But put ye on the Lord Jesus Christ, and make not provision for the flesh, to fulfil the lusts thereof.

ROMANS 13:14

I beseech you therefore, brethren, by the mercies of God, that ye present your bodies a living sacrifice, holy, acceptable unto God, which is your reasonable service.

ROMANS 12:1

And beside this, giving all diligence, add to your faith virtue; and to virtue knowledge. And to knowledge temperance; and to temperance patience; and to patience godliness.

2 PETER 1:6

Be sober, be vigilant; because your adversary the devil, as a roaring lion, walketh about, seeking whom he may devour.

1 PETER 5:8

Let your moderation be known unto all men. The Lord is at hand.

PHILIPPIANS 4:5

And beside this, giving all diligence, add to your faith virtue; and to virtue knowledge.
2 PETER 1:5

Therefore let us not sleep, as do others; but let us watch and be sober.
1 THESSALONIANS 5:6

And every man that striveth for the mastery is temperate in all things. Now they do it to obtain a corruptible crown; but we an incorruptible.
1 CORINTHIANS 9:25

Prove all things; hold fast that which is good.
1 THESSALONIANS 5:21

This I say then, Walk in the Spirit, and ye shall not fulfil the lust of the flesh.
GALATIANS 5:16

Know ye not that ye are the temple of God, and that the Spirit of God dwelleth in you?
1 CORINTHIANS 3:16

The aged women likewise, that they be in behaviour as becometh holiness, not false accusers, not given to much wine, teachers of good things.
TITUS 2:3

That the aged men be sober, grave, temperate, sound in faith, in charity, in patience.
TITUS 2:2

Let no man despise thy youth; but be thou an example of the believers, in word, in conversation, in charity, in spirit, in faith, in purity.
1 TIMOTHY 4:12

EPILOGUE

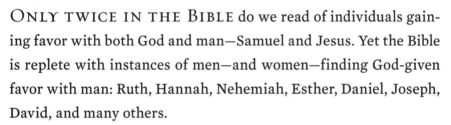

ONLY TWICE IN THE BIBLE do we read of individuals gaining favor with both God and man—Samuel and Jesus. Yet the Bible is replete with instances of men—and women—finding God-given favor with man: Ruth, Hannah, Nehemiah, Esther, Daniel, Joseph, David, and many others.

Teacher and writer Dr. Lance Wallnau has said, "Favor is like being dipped in the honey of God's presence so that all the blessings He has sent start to stick to you!"[69]

When God pours out His favor, it clings like honey and sweetens our actions and interactions with others. It enhances our ability to wait patiently, to smile when things go wrong, and to remain calm when everyone around you is in panic mode. Others are drawn to you because God has given you favor with man.

In Galatians 6:7–9, Paul wrote:

> Do not be deceived, God is not mocked; for whatever a man sows, that he will also reap. For he who sows to his flesh will of the flesh reap corruption, but he who sows to the Spirit will of the Spirit reap everlasting life. And let us not grow weary while doing

good, for in due season we shall reap if we do not lose heart.

These scriptures certainly apply to the seed we sow daily in the lives of men and women—and yes, children—around us. If we allow God to develop the fruit of the Spirit in our lives, we will attract favor with man. That is because what they see will be such a vast departure from the norm. If you sow kindness, you will reap kindness. The same is true of love, joy, peace, and the other godly attributes Jehovah is developing in your life. *God-given* success and favor is dependent on Him alone—not on your talents, skills, good looks, witty tongue, or weighty wallet.

Proverbs 11:27 says, "He who earnestly seeks good finds favor . . . " When we look for the good in the other person, regardless of their attitude toward us, we will find favor—with God and man. Let the love of Christ season every relationship; favor will come. Proverbs 15:1 (NLT) tells us, "A gentle answer deflects anger, but harsh words make tempers flare." Be kind to the pleasant and the unpleasant.

In his book *Favor: The Road to Success*, minister and motivational speaker Bob Buess wrote:

> God is a God of favor, and He is constantly promoting those who learn to live in this law of favor. You draw on this favor in two ways. First, you expect favor to flow from God to you and from others to you. Second, you favor others even when they may not be so kind to you.
>
> God is merciful to the unmerciful. He is kind to the

ugly. He is longsuffering with His enemies. Develop this attitude of praying for your enemy.[70]

In reviewing Luke 2:52 we are reminded that Jesus grew in favor with God and man. Early twentieth-century missionary and author H. C. Trumbull wrote:

> Jesus won the favour of man by seeking the favour of God. It is not so important that man should be pleased with us as that God should. But man's favour is more likely to be won through seeking God's favour than in any other way. If we are always asking how those about us will look at us; if we give large weight in our thoughts to the opinion of our fellows; if we endeavour to so shape our course as to win popular approval, we are by no means sure to have what we strive for; we may fall far short of the coveted favour of man; and, moreover, may utterly lack God's approval, whether man likes or dislikes us. But if we are always asking how God will look at our course; if we give large weight in our thoughts to His opinion and His commandments; if we seek to shape our course to win His approval, we are sure to get what we most long for; and we are surer of having also the favour of man than we could be through any other course. If God is our friend, He can secure to us man's approval. The best of human friends cannot win for us God's favour.[71]

Proverbs 13:15 says, "Good understanding gains favor ..." A discerning heart begets favor with man. People around us are crying to be understood, to be validated by someone. The question becomes, "Do you really see me as a person? Am I just a fixture in your daily routine—a waitress, a clerk, a secretary, a co-worker—or does what I do and say mean something to you? If I were lying wounded on the side of the road, would you stop and offer assistance, or would you simply pass by on the other side?" (See the story of the Good Samaritan in Luke 10:25–37.) Martin Luther King, Jr. said:

> The first question which the priest and the Levite asked was: "If I stop to help this man, what will happen to *me*?" But ... the good Samaritan reversed the question: "If I do not stop to help this man, what will happen to *him*?"[72] (Emphasis added.)

And it was Mother Teresa who said, "We can do no great things, only small things with great love."[73]

Take time to reach out to someone today in love—with a smile, a sincere compliment, a couple of extra dollars as a gratuity for a job well done. When God blesses you with favor with man, use the opportunity to make a significant difference in that person's life.

(Endnotes)

1.   W. F. Adeney, *Expositor's Bible: Ezra, Nehemiah and Esther* (New York: Hodder & Stoughton), N.D.0, 191

2.   http://www.goodreads.com/quotes/600774-there-are-three-types-of-people-in-this-world-those; accessed November 2014.

3.   Donald K. Campbell, *Nehemiah: Man in Charge* (Wheaton, IL: Victor Books, 1981), 71–72.

4.   Compiled by Callie L. Bonney, *The Wisdom and Eloquence of Daniel Webster* (New York: John B. Alden, 1996), 28–29. http://archive.org/stream/wisdomandeloque00websgoog/wisdomandeloque00websgoog_djvu.txt; accessed November 2014.

5.   John Piper, "The Son of God at 12 Years Old," January 12, 1981, http://www.desiringgod.org/sermons/the-son-of-god-at-12-years-old; accessed November 2014.

6.   http://crossquotes.org/category/christmas/; accessed January 2015.

7.   Mary Coyle Chase, author of Harvey, http://www.inspirational-quotes-and-quotations.com/movie-quote-by-james-stewart.html; accessed November 2014.

8.   Ibid.

9.   *Strong's Concordance*, Reference G3586, Blue Letter Bible.com, http://www.blbclassic.org/lang/lexicon/lexicon.cfm?Strongs=G3586&t=KJV; accessed November 2014.

10.   Dr. Max Lucado, "An Encouraging Word from Max Lucado: Joseph," September 30, 2013, http://www.faithgateway.com/what-was-meant-for-evil-god-uses-for-good/#.VH4jCo10w3E; accessed December 2014.

11.   Rev. Bill Versteeg, "Insane or Profoundly Raitonal," http://www.pbv.thunder-bay.on.ca/NetSermons/1Sam21ser.html; accessed December 2014.

12.   Rev. Paul Aiello, Jr., http://www.sermonsearch.com/sermon-illustrations/3911/lighthouse/; accessed November 2014.

13.   Francis Maitland Balfour, http://www.quotationspage.com/quotes/Francis_Maitland_Balfour/; accessed December 2014.

14.   Charles R. Swindoll, http://www.insight.org/resources/articles/encouragement-healing/amazing-grace-on-display.html?t=bible-characters#sthash.FluTSV5s.dpuf; accessed December 2014.

15.   John Eckhardt, "Learn How to Get God's Favor," January 3, 2013, *Charisma Magazine*, http://www.charismamag.com/spirit/spiritual-growth/13392-hunting-gods-goodwill; accessed December 2014.

16.   *Prayers That Avail Much*, Word Ministries, Inc., (Atlanta, GA: Harrison House, 1980.) http://www.prayers.org/prayers/For_Favor.asp; accessed December 2014.

17.   http://thinkexist.com/quotations/integrity/; accessed December 2014.

18.   Gerald Sittser, *A Grace Disguised*, quoted in John Ortberg's *The Life You've Always Dreamed Of* (Grand Rapids, MI: Zondervan, 2002), 211.

19.   Vance Havner, http://www.goodreads.com/quotes/97169-god-uses-broken-things-it-takes-broken-soil-to-produce; accessed December 2014.

20. http://asuccessfuljourney.com/financial/fb2.htm; accessed December 2014.

21. Mark Hall, Casting Crowns - Does Anybody Hear Her Lyrics | MetroLyrics, http://www.metrolyrics.com/does-anybody-hear-her-lyrics-casting-crowns.html; accessed December 2014.

22. http://www.ecclesia.org/truth/smile.html; accessed December 2014.

23. Public domain.

24. http://quotations.about.com/od/funnyquotes/a/smile.htm; accessed December 2014.

25. Michael P. Nichols, *The Lost Art of Listening* (New York: Guilford Press, 1995), 11.

26. Paul Tournier, *To Understand Each Other,* quoted in Charles Swindoll, *Growing Strong in the Seasons of Life* (Portland: Multnomah Press, 1983), 61.

27. Ibid.

28. http://www.quotegarden.com/optimism.html; accessed December 2014.

29. Eugene H. Peterson, *Leap Over A Wall: Earthly Spirituality for Everyday Christians* (New York, NY: Harper Collins, 1998), 160.

30. Ibid, 161.

31. http://www.lyricsmode.com/lyrics/d/dionne_warwick/what_the_world_needs_now.html; accessed January 2015.

32. http://en.wikipedia.org/wiki/Agape; accessed January 2015.

33. Paul L. Tan, *Encyclopedia of 7,700 Illustrations: Signs of the Times* (Garland TX: Bible Communications, 1996), 706.

34. Lily Hardy Hammond, *In the Garden of Delight* (New York: Thomas Y. Crowell Co. 1916), 209.

35. http://en.wikipedia.org/wiki/Pay_it_forward#cite_note-Hammond-1; accessed January 2015.

36. Dominique Mosbergen, "Dads Leave Beloved Crossing Guard Totally Speechless With Wonderful Christmas Surprise," *Huffington Post,* December 19, 2014, http://www.huffingtonpost.com/2014/12/19/crossing-guard-car-dads-nathaniel-kendrick-dallas_n_6355906.html; accessed December 2014.

37. Dr. Billy Graham, "A Simple Message," http://billygraham.org/devotion/a-simple-message/; accessed January 2015.

38. *Albert's Sermon Illustrations,* "The Patrick Henry Hughes Story," http://aksermonillustrations.blogspot.com/search/label/Joy; accessed January 2015.

39. http://www.faithvillage.com/blogpost/85782b12043e4252a7d982eeee15e44e/why_christians_should_smile_more#sthash.B7DvRm1X.dpuf; accessed January 2015.

40. Tryon Edwards, *A Dictionary of Thoughts* (Ann Arbor, MI: F.B. Dickerson and Co., 1908), 533.

41. http://www.scrapbook.com/poems/doc/7590.html#EKcWzoxOec2ERbIC.99; accessed January 2015.

42. Charles Swindoll, "A Reason to Smile," http://www.insight.org/resources/articles/christian-living/reason-to-smile.html?l=fruit-of-the-spirit; accessed January 2015.

43. Rev. John F. Barham, "The Peace of God," http://www.fumctavares.com/files/ Download/080413.pdf; accessed January 2015.

44. "Story from church history: Polycarp burned at the stake," February 23, 2012, *The Voice of the Martyrs*, http://vomcblog.blogspot.com/2012/02/story-from-church-history-polycarp.html; accessed January 2015.

45. By John Piper. ©2015 Desiring God Foundation. Website: desiringGod.org, http://www. desiringgod.org/sermons/my-peace-i-give-to-you-let-not-your-hearts-be-troubled; accessed January 2015.

46. Ibid.

47. http://thinkexist.com/quotation/what_lies_behind_us_and_what_lies_before_us_are/10712. html; accessed January 2015.

48. http://www.brainyquote.com/quotes/topics/topic_patience5.html; accessed January 2015.

49. Rev. Peter Elvin, "Deacon Philip and the Ethiopian Eunuch," http://elvinsermons.blogspot. com/2009/05/deacon-philip-and-ethiopian-eunuch.html; accessed January 2015.

50. Elizabeth George, *Beautiful in God's Eyes: The Treasures of the Proverbs 31 Woman* (Eugene, OR: Harvest House Publishers, 2005), 53

51. Stephanie Sarkis, "50 Quotes on Beauty," *Psychology Today*, April 30, 2012, http://www. psychologytoday.com/blog/here-there-and-everywhere/201204/50-quotes-beauty; accessed January 2015.

52. Paul Lee Tan, 1,457

53. J. Dobson & Gary Bauer, *Children at Risk*, (Nashville, TN: Word Publishing, 1990), 187–188.

54. Pastor Jimmy Dean, First Baptist Church, Barberville, FL, http://www.barberville.net/ sermon112.htm; accessed January 2015

55. *All the Women of the Bible*, Chapter 2. Alphabetical Exposition of Named Bible Women, R— Rizpah, https://www.biblegateway.com/resources/all-women-bible/Rizpah; accessed January 2015.

56. John Piper, "Blessed Are the Meek," February 9, 1986, ©2015 Desiring God Foundation, http:// www.desiringgod.org/sermons/blessed-are-the-meek; accessed January 2015.

57. Ibid.

58. Peter A. Stern, "The World is an Angry Place: Political, Social and Economic Unrest Spreading Throughout the World," August 8, 2011, http://theuniverseatyourfeet.blogspot.com/2011/08/ world-is-angry-place-political-and.html; accessed January 2015.

59. A. W. Tozer, The Pursuit of God (Bialobrzegi, Poland 2014), eBook.

60. http://www.searchquotes.com/quotation/Life_is_a_competition._Survival_of_the_ fittest%2C_fight_for_what_you_want_or_someone_else_will_take_it/427163/; accessed January 2015.

61. Dr. Spiros Zodhiates (Editor) *Complete Word Study Dictionary: New Testament* (Chattanooga, TN: AMG Publishers, 1992), 1,209–1,210.

62. Carolyn Arends, "Strength in Meekness: What to do with the anger that saps strength," *Christianity Today,* February 15, 2010, http://www.christianitytoday.com/ct/2010/ february/20.56.html; accessed January 2015.

63. http://www.goodreads.com/quotes/tag/self-control; accessed January 2015.

64. http://en.wikipedia.org/wiki/Nazirite; accessed January 2015.

65. Alan Sipress, "Death at an Alabama Exit," *Washington Post*, November 16, 1999, http://www. washingtonpost.com/wp-srv/WPcap/1999-11/16/069r-111699-idx.html; accessed January 2015.

66. http://www.brainyquote.com/quotes/quotes/h/harrystrum121205. html#XdMS9J6Fxs2afY6Y.99; accessed January 2015.

67. Allen Randolph, "Favor with God and Man," May 5, 2011, http://www.allenrandolph. com/?p=3360; accessed January 2015.

68. Charles Swindoll, *Growing Strong in the Seasons of Life* (Portland, OR: Multnomah Press, 1983), 276–277.

69. Dr. Lance Wallnau, "Favor," 1989, audiocassette, http://www.amazon.com/FAVOR-DR-LANCE-WALLNAU/dp/B001DK08EO/ref=sr_1_18?s=books&ie=UTF8&qid=1421873646&sr=1-18&keywords=lance+wallnau; accessed January 2015.

70. Bob Buess, *Favor: The Road to Success* (New Kensington, PA: Whitaker House, 1975), 57.

71. H.C. Trumbull, "God's favour to be sought," http://biblehub.com/commentaries/illustrator/ luke/2.htm; accessed January 2015.

72. http://www.quotegarden.com/helping.html; accessed January 2015.

73. Ibid.

MICHAEL DAVID EVANS, the #1 *New York Times* bestselling author, is an award-winning journalist/Middle East analyst. Dr. Evans has appeared on hundreds of network television and radio shows including *Good Morning America, Crossfire* and *Nightline,* and *The Rush Limbaugh Show,* and on Fox Network, *CNN World News,* NBC, ABC, and CBS. His articles have been published in the *Wall Street Journal, USA Today, Washington Times, Jerusalem Post* and newspapers worldwide. More than twenty-five million copies of his books are in print, and he is the award-winning producer of nine documentaries based on his books.

Dr. Evans is considered one of the world's leading experts on Israel and the Middle East, and is one of the most sought-after speakers on that subject. He is the chairman of the board of the Ten Boom Holocaust Museum in Haarlem, Holland, and is the founder of Israel's first Christian museum—Friends of Zion: Heroes and History—in Jerusalem.

Dr. Evans has authored a number of books including: *History of Christian Zionism, Showdown with Nuclear Iran, Atomic Iran, The Next Move Beyond Iraq, The Final Move Beyond Iraq,* and *Countdown.* His body of work also includes the novels *Seven Days, GameChanger, The Samson Option, The Four Horsemen, The Locket, Born Again: 1967,* and coming soon, *The Columbus Code.*

✦ ✦ ✦

Michael David Evans is available to speak or for interviews.
Contact: EVENTS@drmichaeldevans.com.

BOOKS BY: MIKE EVANS

Israel: America's Key to Survival

Save Jerusalem

The Return

Jerusalem D.C.

Purity and Peace of Mind

Who Cries for the Hurting?

Living Fear Free

I Shall Not Want

Let My People Go

Jerusalem Betrayed

Seven Years of Shaking: A Vision

The Nuclear Bomb of Islam

Jerusalem Prophecies

Pray For Peace of Jerusalem

America's War: The Beginning
of the End

The Jerusalem Scroll

The Prayer of David

The Unanswered Prayers of Jesus

God Wrestling

The American Prophecies

Beyond Iraq: The Next Move

The Final Move beyond Iraq

Showdown with Nuclear Iran

Jimmy Carter: The Liberal Left
and World Chaos

Atomic Iran

Cursed

Betrayed

The Light

Corrie's Reflections & Meditations

GAMECHANGER SERIES:
GameChanger
Samson Option
The Four Horsemen

THE PROTOCOLS SERIES:
The Protocols
The Candidate

The Revolution

The Final Generation

Seven Days

The Locket

Living in the F.O.G.

Persia: The Final Jihad

Jerusalem

The History of Christian Zionism

Countdown

Ten Boom: Betsie, Promise of God

Commanded Blessing

Born Again: 1948

Born Again: 1967

Presidents in Prophecy

Stand with Israel

Prayer, Power and Purpose

Turning Your Pain Into Gain

Christopher Columbus, Secret Jew

Finding Favor with God

Finding Favor with Man

The Jewish State: The Volunteers

See You in New York

COMING SOON:

The Columbus Code

Friends of Zion

TO PURCHASE, CONTACT: orders@timeworthybooks.com
P. O. BOX 30000, PHOENIX, AZ 85046